p. 41
p. 109
Epilogue 1

enough

enough

*Finding abundant life
in a world striving for more*

elise knobloch

*Author from Sioux Falls, S.D.
Spa Day 1/26/2019
Led by Marci Doll*

encouragemeup.com

ISBN-13: 978-1973919612

Author photo credit: Crista Ballard
Editors: Tracy Kirby and Cynthia Epp
Design: Tim Murray, paperbackdesign.com

For more information or to order additional copies please visit encouragemeup.com.

Lord, You have assigned me my portion and my cup;
You have made my lot secure. The boundary lines
have fallen for me in pleasant places; surely I have a
delightful inheritance.

Psalm 16:5-6

Introduction
Gathering Enough: Manna from Heaven

Epilogue

Introduction

"I've had ENOUGH!" That declaration right there is frequently how my kids know Mom is tapping out. I am done with my day. The final reserve I had stored up to get the wee ones tucked into their beds has been depleted, and the kids are left to fend for themselves. Mom is headed to the bathtub. After all, the kids have all had their bath time (at some point in the last seven days, I mean), and now it's my turn. Peace out. I will see you mañana.

As if it were that easy. As if I could just give up and walk away. Inevitably, one of my husband's precocious offspring will miss the obvious social cue that my day is done and will hunt me down to make one last request. Usually for a drink of water. Or seven. Camels these children become at bedtime. Little rascals.

I love being Mom to these four little rascal camels. I want them to want me. I want to be their go-to person. Just not after 8 p.m., or when I have other things

1

I need to be doing. Or want to be doing. Or think I need to be doing, but really probably only want to be doing. Even though I claim to be done with my day, in actuality, part of me feels like *my* day only really begins once they are all sleeping. Only at that time do I feel like I get to do what I want, with whatever energy I have left.

And yet, in those quiet moments, as I reflect on the day behind and the week ahead, so often I find myself thinking about them, and me, and my husband, and my job, and our home, and my friends, and my friends' homes, and how this whole thing called "Life" is shaping up. And doubt creeps in again.

Am I doing enough for my kids' development? We should limit their time on the iPad more. Then Drew would know his alphabet, right? I am not doing enough to develop my career. What is a part-time lawyer anyway? Man, I haven't played with my kids enough. I might as well be working full-time for as often as I play ball tag with the boys. And I haven't provided enough structure for them. If I'm not playing with them, I should at least be teaching them how to be productive. Which reminds me, I am not volunteering enough. Here I am worrying about my family who has everything we need, and I should be helping those who do not. It's probably because I'm not reading my Bible enough.

How can I be this tired and still feel like I haven't done enough?

Then I think about all the roles to which God has called me, and other women like me. It helps explain the exhaustion. And then I start to doubt my abilities in these different roles. (Good times in the bathtub, let me tell you—very relaxing.) Sure, I am called into all these different roles, but I don't have what I need to do any of them well. I am not compassionate enough to be a Christian. I am not patient enough to be a mother. I am not homemakery enough to stay at home. I am not smart enough to be a lawyer. I am not witty enough to be a writer.

How can I be called to be all these things and not be enough at any of them?

I don't want to be like this. I want to do Life well, but I don't want to go through life constantly thinking, *Pull it together, girl.* I don't want to be this tired and not feel like I'm winning in some way, but rather losing myself in the process.

Women have more opportunities than ever—for our careers, for our kiddos, for our self-improvement, for our biblical study—and countless resources to help us thrive. We have Pinterest for crying out loud. We have everything earthly possible to be so good at any and everything we want to be. Or feel like we need to be. Or that everyone else is good at.

And yet so many of us feel as though something is missing. Or, that we are missing something.

That "something" may be a lack of fulfilling purpose or a small voice nagging that we or our work don't matter. Perhaps we have unmet expectations of what life would be at this stage of the game, or of how marriage would work or of when marriage would happen, or of how fulfilling parenting would always feel. Perhaps we see one carefully-selected snippet of how another is living which creates a lingering moment of frustration that they seem to have it all together and it's confidence-wrecking that the uncut and unedited documentary of our own life does not look equally unique and interesting.

Maybe you can't put your finger on it. Perhaps you simply get to the end of your day after running around, being so stinking intentional about all of it, and you find yourself asking the question:

How can life be this full and yet, so often I feel unfulfilled?

I can relate. I am tired of feeling discontent. At thirty-plus years old, I want to be comfortable in my own skin, and I want to enjoy the simple pleasures of my own life. Why is all of this never enough?

Jesus said, "The thief comes only to steal and kill and destroy; I have come that they may have life, and have it to the full."[1] I want what Jesus is offering—life to the full. But so often I only feel like I am living a full life. I want back what the thief has stolen, killed, or destroyed which is holding me back from life to the full.

That thief is a sneaky little devil. (Literally.) He doesn't often steal large amounts of joy, peace, love— whatever it is—all at once. He "salami slices" it. Are you familiar with that term? Salami slicing is a method of stealing an unnoticeable amount—perhaps fractions of a penny—over an extended period of time. Those small, nearly imperceptible amounts can add up over time to a huge sum without the victim ever knowing they have been robbed. I am sick of Satan salami slicing away at my contentment and confidence as a child of God. I want it all back.

I want to be content in the life I am living, or to

---

1 John 10:10. Unless otherwise noted, all scripture references are from the NIV Bible.

start living a life in which I am content.

There is a heavenly battle over the contentment of our souls and the actions of our lives. Satan is subtle and persistent, but not overly novel. He attacks those areas of our lives that God intends to be fulfilling—our relationships, our vocations, our gifts, our confidence as a child of God—and attempts to make our perception of them into something less than. Less than what we thought it would be, less than what others have, less than what we expected for ourselves.

Sometimes he subtly attacks our perception of ourselves, planting just enough doubt to shift our confidence off-kilter. Perhaps he attacks the value of our gifts and vocations with which God intends us to bless others. He encourages us to look sideways at our neighbors, loved ones, televisions, social media accounts, and start comparing what He has given us with what He has given others. And then Satan whispers: *You are not that. You don't have that. But you could. Be more like them. Work a bit harder. Don't settle. Keep striving.*

Anything he can do to turn our eyes from God the Father.

This is not a new tactic by the Father of Lies. He knows that over time, salami-sliced contentment turns slowly into discontentment, and it rubs against our created state—our most authentic self—which longs to rest contentedly with our Creator. Satan, however, loves to exploit that basic human desire for more, quietly taunting: *You got this, all by yourself.*

But we don't got this, all by ourselves. We were not created that way. Nevertheless, as we head out on our independent journey, unconsciously striving toward something more, toward something different, we start to lose sight of who we were created to be and of what we were created to do. We lose sight of our uniqueness because we start comparing and contending for that which seems more desirable. For that which seems more interesting, more witty, more important, more purposeful in our perception of the lives others are living. We stop living our authentic lives, and discontent spirals downward. The thief is a sneaky little devil indeed.

THE DAY THE LORD WHISPERED the concept of "Enough" into my ear, I had been working so hard to ignore the negative script that had been playing loudly in my head for the few days before. My self-confidence had been stripped. My parenting sucked. I felt like I wasn't doing anything well. I felt directionless. Over the last eight years, God had been prompting me to write a book, and I had felt an incredible sense of urgency for the few weeks before to get it done. And by get it done, I really mean get it started. I had given a rough draft of a book idea to an editor, but we both knew something was missing. It was a frustrated sense of urgency because I didn't know how to fix it. I needed more expertise. I needed something more interesting, more profound, more witty to say. What I had wasn't enough. I stood in front of the mirror, make-up only partly applied on my face, wondering how one applied mascara when the tears wouldn't stop. I was paralyzed by the script of defeat running through my mind. That's when God, as clear as day, had a word for me: "Enough!" I stood still, listening, the destructive dialogue in my head temporarily silenced. The message was deliberate, firm but gentle: "Enough! My grace is enough."

Enough. As I let that word sink in and push the negative script out of my head, that word began to encapsulate not only the problem, but also the answer I was so desperately searching for. God wanted to have a word with me about my contentment and what I was doing to find it. And how I was losing myself—my authenticity—in the process. I was seeking to do more to find it, and His word—Enough!—commanded me to stop and be still. I was seeking to get more for myself and His word was an unequivocal reminder that He provided the exact amount—the enough—that I needed. And perhaps above all, His one word reminded me that He is always sufficient—always enough—for me.

God always provides enough for my never-enoughs.

THERE YOU HAVE IT. That's the point of this book. We restore our contentment when we live authentically within the space of knowing that we will never be enough, but that God always will be. I need Him in order to be most-fully me. What I wrestled with for eight years, the Holy Spirit formatted in one simple statement that spoke straight to my heart. God created the world, and creates life, so I suppose the book format was pretty doable for Him. But, it sure impressed me.

He wasn't done. That afternoon, I started Internet research on where "enough" was found in the Bible. Within ten minutes, I felt overwhelmed and defeated again because nothing was standing out as something interesting I could write about. (Patience is a virtue, just not one of mine.) The need for more of my abilities was starting to creep in again. In frustration, I opened my Bible to where I had left off in John 14 as I had been reading through the Bible over the last number of years. Before I read, I breathed a quick prayer for God to show me what He had for me. Within thirty seconds my eyes sat glued on John 14:8—"Philip said, 'Lord, show us the Father and that will be *enough* for us.'" There was that word again. Enough. Even as I struggled in my not enough, He provided. He put before me the clear, unequivocal focus of my writing: Just show them the Father and that is enough. Anything of eternal value always points back to the Father. My purpose with this book is to point you to the Father to allow Him to show you Enough. Who needs the Internet when you have the One who breathed it to show you?

THAT WAS THE BEGINNING of my journey with Enough. Very quickly as I studied "enough" in scripture, I wandered upon the story of the Israelites wandering in the desert, gathering manna. I have heard and read the story of manna many times, but the use of the word "enough" in its telling has opened my eyes to understand its significance in an entirely different way. It is, fittingly, the biblical story of gathering enough for each day. This provision of manna uniquely illustrates God's daily, exactly-perfect provision to a wandering people searching for something more, for something promised to them. People just like us.

THE HEBREWS LEARNED SO MUCH as they wandered as a tribe in the desert journeying to draw closer and depend on God. I have learned so much from the tribe with which I wander as well. The lessons from the Hebrews apply to me and my tribe, and hopefully to you and yours, still today. Human nature is funny; while culture and circumstances may change, some elements of the human experience never will.

The Bible is the living, breathing Word of God. You can practically watch the pages rise and fall like the chest of a sleeping child, which is an equally angelic picture, isn't it?[2] And as it turns out, if a person (say for example, me) allows God to show her what the living Bible has to say about "enough"—which may take more than ten minutes—that person may be transformed. It's true. Spending time in His Word, focused on one word, was enough to show me more of Him. And nothing transforms more than seeing more of the Father. Hang with me, and be encouraged and transformed by His Word too.

I am not offering a guaranteed 3-step process to contentment with this book; I'm offering to be a travel partner. I trust that as I show you the Father, He will show you what "Enough" is in your life. My prayer for this book is much like the apostle Paul's to the church of Ephesus: **that you will "grasp how wide and long and high and deep is the love of Christ" for you.**[3] **And that you may be "filled to the measure of all the fullness of God."**[4] Not to be bossy, but please read that

---

2 Sidenote: How many days is the struggle of parenthood instantly redeemed by the sight of a sleeping child? I used to wonder why parents watched their kids sleep; now I get it—it's God's way of getting us to show up again in the morning.
3 Ephesians 3:18
4 Ephesians 3:19

again. Filled to the measure of all the fullness of God. That right there is living life to the full. That right there is filling in what has been salami sliced away. That right there ... is His Enough for you.

Gathering Enough:
Manna from Heaven

LET ME SET THE SCENE: the Hebrews had been in slavery under the Egyptians for several hundred years. They cried out to the Lord, but He was seemingly unmoved to help. Generation after generation of Hebrews pleaded with the Lord to deliver them from oppression as they slaved day by day, surviving back-breaking labor, enduring edicts that demanded the killing of their baby boys, and suffering the agony of feeling separated from their God. But then, He sent Moses.

The Lord gave Moses a purpose—he was to lead the Israelites out of slavery in Egypt and away from the oppression of Pharaoh. Moses felt inadequate as a speaker and God allowed his brother Aaron to go along and help speak to Pharaoh. Initially when Moses and Aaron approached Pharaoh and asked him to allow the Hebrews to leave so that they might worship the Lord, Pharaoh refused and thus the plagues began. Following rivers of blood, gobs of frogs, gnasty gnats (the "g" is silent in both), incessant insects, dead livestock, festering boils, horrendous hail, lingering locusts, endless darkness, and the death of the Egyptians' firstborn sons, Pharaoh finally relented and allowed the Israelites to leave Egypt.[1] Do not mess with the will of God for His people.

Moses and Aaron led the Israelites into the desert and away from slavery, but then the people got hungry. And when people get hungry, they become irrational. I get it. They wanted food. So the Hebrews started grumbling that it would have been better if they had stayed in slavery in Egypt because there at least they "sat around pots of meat and ate all the food [they] wanted."[2] Never mind that whole slavery dilemma. God had a herd of hangry Hebrews on His hands.

So, how did Father God respond? He provided. The Lord heard their grumbling and said to Moses:

> "I will rain down bread from heaven for you. The people are to go out each day and gather **enough** for that day. In this way I will test them and see if they will follow my instructions. On the sixth day they are to prepare what they bring in, and that is to be twice as much as they gather on the other days."
>
> The Lord said to Moses, "I have heard the grumbling of the Israelites. Tell them, 'At twilight you will eat meat, and in the morning you will be filled with bread. Then you will

---

1 I encourage you to read this more in depth in Exodus 3—15.
2 Exodus 16:3

know that I am the Lord your God.'"

That evening quail came and covered the camp, and in the morning there was a layer of dew around the camp. When the dew was gone, thin flakes like frost on the ground appeared on the desert floor. When the Israelites saw the quail and manna from heaven, they said to each other, "What is it?" For they did not know what it was.

Moses said to them, "It is the bread the Lord has given you to eat. This is what the Lord has commanded: 'Each one is to gather as much as he needs.'"

The Israelites did as they were told; some gathered much, some little. And when they measured it...he who gathered much did not have too much, and he who gathered little did not have too little. Each one gathered as much as he needed.

Then Moses said to them, "No one is to keep any of it until morning."[3]

This is God's story of teaching His people to gather Heaven's gift of enough.

_____

3 Exodus 16:4-5, 11-19

provision

"Go out each day and gather enough."

First of all, it is worth noting that the Israelites' roadtrip hunger meltdown took place six weeks into a forty-year journey. To put that into perspective, if the journey had been a four-hour car trip, this is equivalent to your children starting to complain forty-one seconds into the trip. I don't know about you, but that sounds about right for us.

Moses instructed the Israelites to "go out each day and gather enough for that day."[1] In the original language, the Hebrew word for "enough" in this passage means "the matter" or "the thing" for the day, but is often translated as "the portion for the day," or the "day's portion." The Hebrew idiom in this passage

---

1 Exodus 16:4

reads as "the matter of a day in its day."[2]

This phrase was so familiar to the Hebrews, it may have caused them to shudder. The Egyptian taskmasters used this phrase in dictating the daily quota of bricks they were required to make under Pharaoh. In Exodus 5, Moses and Aaron had asked Pharaoh to allow the Hebrews to travel to the desert to worship God. As you read Pharaoh's response, take careful notice of how he treated those under his authority. Later, we will contrast that with Yahweh's way.

> Moses and Aaron came and said to Pharaoh, "Thus says the Lord, the God of Israel, 'Let my people go that they may celebrate a feast to Me in the wilderness....'" But the king of Egypt said to them, "Moses and Aaron, why do you draw the people away from their work? Get back to your labors!" Again Pharaoh said, "Look, the people of the land are now many, and you would have them cease from their labors!" So the same day Pharaoh commanded the taskmasters over the people and their foremen, saying, "You are no longer to give the people straw to make brick as previously; let them go and gather straw for themselves. But the quota of bricks which they were making previously, you shall impose on them; you are not to reduce any of it. Because they are

---

2 S. R. Driver, *The Cambridge Bible for Schools and Colleges: Exodus* (Cambridge: Cambridge University Press, 1911), http://biblehub.com/commentaries/cambridge/exodus/5.htm. See commentary on Exodus 5:13.

lazy, therefore they cry out, 'Let us go and sacrifice to our God.' Let the labor be heavier on the men, and let them work at it so that they will pay no attention to false words."

So the taskmasters of the people and their foremen went out and spoke to the people, saying, "Thus says Pharaoh, 'I am not going to give you any straw. You go and get straw for yourselves wherever you can find it, but none of your labor will be reduced.'" So the people scattered through all the land of Egypt to gather stubble for straw. The taskmasters pressed them, saying, "Complete your work quota, your daily amount, just as when you had straw."[3]

This quota, "your daily amount," is that same phrase—"the matter of a day in its day." Let's spend a little time unpacking that phrase as well as the significance of who has the authority to dictate that "matter of a day in its day" in our lives.

Moses and Aaron desired to carry out God's spoken purpose for the Hebrews to allow them to worship God. Pharaoh, however, could not fathom that all of those workers would "cease from their labors." What sense did that make for all of the workers to stop working and worship God? Who would get the all-important work done then? *What a nonsensical request*, Pharaoh thought. Pharaoh believed the request to worship was disguised

---

3 Exodus 5:1, 4-13 (New American Standard Bible)

laziness, and he wouldn't stand for it. He believed the Hebrews had gone soft, too much in the way of straw had been provided to them, so he ordered that the slaves gather their own straw. He wanted the work to be so much that it would distract them from other things—the "false words" of Moses and Aaron offering worship.

We face this every day in our lives too, don't we? Yes, it would be great if we had the time daily to spend worshiping God, spending time in His Word, asking Him to dictate our purpose in each day. But who has the time—we have too much to do, don't we?

Why is it so difficult for us to make time for God?

In the famous words of Saturday Night Live's Church Lady, "could it be...Satan?" Of course it is. Matthew Henry's Concise Commentary says this about Pharaoh's response: "The malice of Satan has often represented the service and worship of God as fit employment only for those who have nothing else to do, and the business only of the idle."[4] Regardless of what we have to do in a day, or what we have already accomplished, Satan would love to thwart what God would have us do each day. He loves to suggest that we don't have enough time to worship, to study God's Word, to share a story with our children, to be there for a friend. Satan would have us believe that our self-proclaimed purposes need to be the priority. *Important people are too busy*, he taunts. The Father of Lies loves for us to believe that we have not yet done enough with our day; perhaps others are doing more? *Do more to be more*, he lies. Perhaps above all, Satan

---

4 Matthew Henry, *Matthew Henry's Concise Commentary*, N.p., 1706, http://biblehub.com/commentaries/mhc/exodus/5.htm.

would love for us to believe that not only do we have more important things that need to get done, but to take time to worship our Creator—in whatever form that might take—is laziness.

Did you notice any difference in the way Pharaoh demonstrated authority compared to how God did? When Pharaoh had authority over the Hebrews, he demanded they work all the time. In fact, because they asked to worship their God, he withheld resources he had previously provided, thereby requiring them to work harder. His human wisdom could not understand the value of worship and he responded by creating more work. Umm...yeah. I do that too. I elevate work over worship. At times, I even create "good" work to impress God, when what He really desires is my worship. My days get full with my labors.

When God had authority over the Hebrews however, He desired for them to have opportunity to rest and worship Him. So while listening to them grumble and complain, He responded by providing everything they needed. In fact, He also created a day of rest, during which they wouldn't have to do more work, but would be able to focus solely on worshiping Him. (We'll come back to how some responded to that opportunity to rest later on. We humans are so funny. And by funny, I mean foolish.)

Question: Is your memory better than the Grumbling Hangry Hebrews? They seem to have forgotten all about the back-breaking ceaseless labor that had them trudging throughout Egypt looking for stubbles of straw. Apparently, stew meat trumped freedom. That seems like such a ridiculous trade off to me, but if I'm honest, I tend to have the same tendencies in my own life. I am always looking for ways to feel filled up. Moments of instant gratification that make me feel satisfied. But like stew meat, they don't fill up for long, and the hungry, unsatisfied feeling comes back. So, I seek more of something that will quickly satisfy. Maybe it's a thing. Maybe it's a feeling. Often, it's chocolate. But whatever it is, it isn't enough to fulfill for long. It doesn't offer contentment. **If we aren't looking to Jesus to fill us up, those things that threaten to enslave us begin to regain their appeal.**

GOD BROKE THE EGYPTIANS' CHAINS of slavery and in one historical moment gave the Hebrews their physical independence. But they were in bondage in more ways than their daily brick requirements. Providing their one-time independence was not His ultimate purpose (although they may have thought it was). God wanted His people to depend on Him, to draw close to Him, to be filled in a way stew meat never could.

Can we take a moment to point out what God didn't do to provide food for the Israelites? God did not replenish their stockpile of provisions. He could have dropped an abundance of provisions for the Israelites to haul around. Certainly, then they would have known they had enough, even if it was a burden to carry around. He could have rained down ten different ingredients with a recipe to follow—after all, He wanted to see if they could follow instructions. He might have gotten creative and given half of the camp certain ingredients and the other half other ingredients and turned meal prep into a team-building exercise. But, He didn't.

No, the team-building exercise He chose was the Trust Fall: They had to trust that the food would fall. Day after day. The Israelites were wholly dependent on God's provision and the provision was specific to that day. His trustworthiness would appear before them in the dew of the next day as they gathered the matter of the day in its day once again. Through manna, God began laying the groundwork by which the Israelites would learn to depend on Him consistently. Day after day. Dependence is necessarily a short-term, ongoing thing, isn't it? Without a frequent, continual reminder of a need and the continual provision that meets that need, it starts to feel less like dependence.

Some of the Hebrews however, were slow learners, or resourceful, depending on your perspective. They thought they would cheat the day-by-day system with what they assumed would be a "work smarter, not harder" approach. Observe:

> Then Moses said to them, "No one is to keep any of it until morning." However, some of them paid no attention to Moses; they kept part of it until morning, but it was full of maggots and began to smell. So Moses was angry with them. Each morning everyone gathered as much as he needed, and when the sun grew hot, it melted away.[5]

Two things, and then I will get back to my point: First of all, how many of you drive kids around in a mini-van? I do. And you cannot make me go to the very

5 Exodus 16:19-21

back row of seats. Know why? The cup holders. Those petri dishes of nastiness most certainly resemble and smell like day-old manna did. And boy does that smelly crustiness make me angry. Do not get me started on when they leave milk back there. (You need not bother to ask who gives them the milk back there in the first place. It just is what it is, people.)

Second, I would never go out to eat if at the end of a meal at home, when everyone had had their fill, the leftover mess simply melted away. Are you kidding me? Just to be clear: God was offering to provide the food as well as clean up. Why would anyone grumble about a chef and a housekeeper?

But I'm off-track. Here's the point: **Like day-old manna, life stinks when we attempt to maintain our independence; we were created to live in dependence on God.** The Hebrews thought they had gained their independence, but God wanted them to gain so much more. He wanted them to gain freedom in Him. But the freedom He was offering them looked like nothing they would ever be able to achieve on their own. This freedom comes from learning a new way that involves Him intrinsically.

The same is true for us. Our journey is not about learning to gather enough on our own. This journey of life is to live out our purpose of glorifying Him. As we go out each day and gather enough for that day, seeking Him in those moments lays the groundwork for us to learn dependence on Him as well. Our freedom, our ability to live life to the full is borne out of learning to depend more deeply on our Father.

Manna for a Mundane Monday

I WANT MY CHILDREN to grow up to be indepen-dent-thinking, helpful contributors to society. But I'd probably be okay if the helpful-contributor traits de-veloped earlier than the independent-thinking traits for ease of parenting. So far, that has not been the case. We encourage independence because it's import-ant for their development that they learn to do things on their own obviously, but also because I get tired of doing certain things for them. I'll be honest—certain developmental milestones have been achieved at the Knobloch house simply because I. Cannot. Anymore. If my children were able to do certain things like feed-ing themselves at a younger age than "normal," it may have had less to do with them being developmentally advanced and more to do with the lack of patience of their mother. (You will see this as a recurring theme throughout the book. God is not finished with me yet.)

But regardless of motivation, teaching and allow-ing appropriate independence is a legitimate parenting goal, right? We are instructed to "train our children in the way they should go"...and then let them go that way.[1] And when they grow up, they can enjoy all the carefree freedoms of adulthood (snicker, snicker).

Spiritually though, our development is the oppo-

1 Proverbs 22:6

site. Our sinful state positions us independently from God; it creates an innate desire to live apart from God. My motto as a toddler—"I do it self"—served me fine as I grew up and met challenges head on, but that mind-set has not helped me one iota in my spiritual journey. It's through recognizing our need to be dependent on a Savior that we find freedom and growth. Dependence in spiritual growth, much like independence in physical growth, takes some learning. And relearning. Again and again. Thankfully, we have a patient Father.

The idea of freedom through dependence may chafe against those who have an independent nature, like it does mine, but the two are not mutually exclusive. One can be both wholly dependent on God and fiercely independently-natured. There may be some refining work He intends to do, but God can use an independent predisposition for His glory. He calls us to be who we are, but to recognize that who we are is who He has created and called us each to be. His calling comes before our being. Put another way, God has a purpose for all my weird ways; He intends to show me what those are. He will not show me my whole calling at once, but rather provides the matter of the day in its day for me. God provides Enough for me daily as I seek and trust that provision to come, day by day, moment by moment. It's not lazy to be still before God, seeking His enough for me for that time. This is the primary purpose for which I have been created.

As I seek God and seek to be content in the life which He has created for me, the instruction to the Hebrews to gather enough in each day is a reminder to me that I will not see that whole picture at once, and that

I don't need to. I can rest in knowing what I know and in having what I need for that time. It also reminds me not to get distracted on the little details that threaten to salami-slice just a touch of my contentment. The instruction to "go out and gather enough for each day" encourages me to keep an eternal perspective on life.

When I was growing up, my dad didn't offer much advice. He was more likely to make a joke than give a lecture, which mirrored the little advice he did give. His advice was usually in the form of only one of two comments. I heard them most often during the roller-coaster of my teenage years. When I was getting hung up on small, insignificant things that didn't deserve my fretting energy, he would remind me: *Life's too short.* And other times, when I would get overwhelmed by things that seemed too insurmountable (which, as a teenager, may have actually been small, insignificant things), he would reassure me: *Life's a long time.* Leave it to my dad to offer advice that seemingly contradicts itself. In reality, he was offering wonderful, eternal perspective. He was at once lifting my eyes away from the small things of life to see the bigger picture, and showing me that even those things that seem too big are actually usually quite small. For a wise guy, my dad is pretty smart.

THE ISRAELITES, TOO, WERE FOCUSED on the immediate needs and desires in front of them. Their hunger seemed huge. They couldn't yet see the big picture of what God was teaching them about dependence, and at the same time, they got lost in the little details. Hungering for stew meat was not worth slavery. They wanted an instantly-fixed life without doing the day-to-day functions necessary to teach them what they needed to learn. They were at once missing the big picture and missing the little picture, and the result was discontentment and grumbling.

DEPENDENCE IS A BIG PICTURE CONCEPT and a day-to-day obedience in living at the same time. Knowing God is dependable is different than depending on Him to set the daily course of your life. Trusting Him to provide life to the full, as He has promised, is not a one-time guarantee. Life happens one day at a time. In the same way, as we seek to regain the contentment in our lives that Satan has salami-sliced away, we will only find it one way: by keeping an eternal perspective and by living in day-by-day dependence. We regain our contentment the same way the thief takes it: little by little. But rather than losing it unknowingly, we learn to become more conscious in keeping it.

Let me tell you about a precious woman in my tribe whom I sometimes envy and compare myself to. (We will get to the problem with envy and comparison in a later chapter, so I am not yet accountable for those inappropriate responses.) I have a dear friend named Sarah who models for me a woman who is about the work of God. Sarah has a strong desire to stay home with her children. But, she has a stronger desire to serve God and follow His will for her life. For now, God has called her to work outside the home. And work she does. She's an engineer who continues to move up through the management ranks of a publicly-trad-ed manufacturing corporation, where she is currently the Director of Operations of one of their divisions. She's kind of a big deal. One of her many skills that has caused her to promote is her ability to effectively "clean up" various underperforming divisions of the company. She routinely makes difficult, life-affecting decisions for her employees for whom she cares greatly. She has grown weary in times of layoffs and termination meetings, but presses on with her best effort even when improvement is non-apparent and morale is low.

I have asked Sarah, in different times of struggle—whether the struggle stems from an underlying desire to be at home with her kids, or from the stressful nature of her job—how she continues to show up every day and give her best effort. Her reply is classic Sarah: She has made a firm deal with God. It's so adorable to hear her retell these stories of how she talks with God; she is the kindest sweetheart you will ever meet, but she can "go manager" when needed in less than 2.2 seconds. Here's the deal: Sarah will give her best effort in all that her job requires, even those tasks that don't capture her heart, but God has to "show her the eternal" in it; He has to show her why this matters for His kingdom. Before she tackles a task that feels too big for her to accomplish, or performs another mundane managerial meeting, she asks the Lord to show her the eternal in it. He doesn't always, but the discipline of asking helps keep her focused on whom she serves. Seeking the Lord in all things keeps her eyes on Christ and what His purposes in that moment are for her. She depends on God to show her why this moment matters to Him.

Ironically, I sometimes struggle with being at home and see Sarah's job as more praiseworthy and important. Sometimes I envy the clout that comes with being a big deal in the corporate world. (Sarah would laugh at this perception.) But her commitment to look for the eternal in her corporate world tasks, even as she longs to be home with her children, has convicted me to look for the eternal in my household tasks, even as I long to hold social clout. Even as my daily gathering seems to be unraveling. I show the love of Christ to each of my kids as I endlessly wipe noses, hands, and bottoms. She shows the love of Christ as she shakes hands and watches the bottom line. I may not always feel important, and my tasks may feel mundane, but Sarah's perspective reminds me to daily live as someone with an eternal purpose. Asking God to show me what that is reminds me who orders my day.

THE DAILY GATHERING OF MANNA was such a mundane activity, made even more mundane by the fact that it was the *same thing* every single day. The only variety was day six when they had to gather twice as much. *What a special treat,* they must have sarcastically thought. (Have you ever met an ancient Hebrew who wasn't sarcastic?) Couldn't God instead have had Moses hold a daily briefing to reveal where in the desert they were wandering that day? That seems like it would be much more dramatic and interesting. Maybe God knows better than me, though. Perhaps it was important that the lesson happened in the day-to-day monotony of it all. Life-changing lessons often happen within the framework of a mundane Monday.

Tish Harrison Warren, in *Liturgy of the Ordinary*, says this,

> We tend to want a Christian life with the dull bits cut out.
>
> Yet God made us to spend our days in rest, work, and play, taking care of our bodies, our families, our neighborhoods, our homes. What if all these boring parts matter to God? What if days passed in ways that feel small and insignificant to us are weighty with meaning and part of the abundant life that God has for us?[2]

When we decided to sell our house a few years ago, we needed to do some major touch-up painting in the hallway that led to our bedrooms. I set about the work one afternoon. I laughed as I painted over the name "BEN" written in pen just to the left of our bedroom door. I remembered my conversation with Ben when I saw his name there originally, and how he adamantly denied that he had written it. It wasn't until I laid out my entire case—the fact that he was still holding the pen, that he was the only child who knew the letters of the alphabet, and that he had just learned to write his name—that he finally fessed up. I remember how I hated that a child of mine refused to tell me the truth.

Further down the hallway, just above the baseboard trim near the bottom of the wall, I painted over red, blue, and yellow streaks—the result of many drive-by scuffings. All three boys had spent countless hours

---

2 Tish Harrison Warren, *Liturgy of the Ordinary* (Downers Grove, IL: InterVarsity Press, 2016), 22.

tearing up and down that hallway with their prima-ry-colored walkers. Essentially, they had each learned to walk, or more appropriately run, in that hallway. I wondered how many hours I watched them run down the hall, dive onto the bed, run all the way back down the hall and flop on our now-spring-popping couches.

As I painted, I reflected on how much of our dai-ly life had happened in that hallway. Sure, we'd had birthday parties and Christmas mornings in the living room, family get-togethers in the kitchen, and fun movie nights downstairs, but so many day-to-day mo-ments—conversations, playtime adventures, snuggles, meltdowns—took place in that hallway.

That hallway in our house reflects the daily minu-tia of our lives, and is very much like the mundane task of gathering enough manna day in and day out. God often uses the "hallways" of our lives to teach us the biggest lessons and for us to have great impact.

When I think of people who have had the larg-est impact on God's kingdom, I often think of grand conversions and larger-than-life personalities. Cer-tainly, sometimes that's true. But I found this gem in Acts about the apostle Paul. The apostle Paul had been preaching in Thessalonica and Berea but had to leave because his teaching had stirred up mobs against him. He went instead to Athens to wait for Timothy and Silas. In Acts 17:16, it says, "*While Paul was waiting for them in Athens*, he was greatly distressed to see that the city was full of idols. So he reasoned in the synagogue with the Jews and the God-fearing Greeks, as well as in the marketplace *day by day* with those who happened to be there." When the audience began to dispute him, he shared the gospel and several became followers.

Paul made an eternal difference in the lives of multiple people "while he was waiting...in Athens." Big things—eternal things—happen in the in-between day-to-day moments of living life. He who is faithful in little will be faithful in much. God does not reveal the lifetime plan He has for you. Dare I say it would be too big for any one person to take in at once. Lifetime purposes are revealed and lived out one day, one moment, at a time.

As you seek contentment in where God has you, are you taking time to be still and seek the moment by moment manna that He provides?

Perhaps you're thinking, *Oh great. Here it comes. She's going to tell me I need daily quiet time in the Word. Let me guess—it works best if I simply wake up at 5:00 am. All I need to do is set aside a mere two hours every morning, then I'll be okay.* Nope, I'm not going to tell you that, although maybe that's what works for you. If it does, keep doing that. If not, look for other ways to add in the good stuff. Time with God is not a prescription— once a day every day, better in the morning, is not a guarantee. Perhaps you steal moments throughout your day to be still. Have verses around your house, car, or office to pull your mind to better places when you're in the thick of things. Maybe it's practicing to simply stop and ask God to help in all of those moments that fray your sanity. Look for ways to seek fulfillment from the only One who has the nourishment to fulfill. **Your soul's contentment comes not from daily *doing* more for God; it comes from daily *depending* more on God.**

uncertainty

"What is it?"

THERE IS A THEORY in communication studies known as Uncertainty Reduction Theory. The main assumption with the theory is that people feel uncomfortable with uncertainty, particularly as it relates to an unknown relationship, and therefore will begin communicating in order to gather more information about the other person. They are willing to share about themselves because vulnerability encourages the other individual to reciprocate and provide information about themselves. This new information reduces uncertainty and, thus, the discomfort people feel about the unknown.

Our youngest son is the poster child for Uncertainty Reduction Theory; he's an incessant question asker and is always looking to gain information in order to gain comfort about his surroundings and upcoming events. In fact, just the other day Drew asked me what he should do in the event I got arrested and he was with me. I'm glad we've got that highly-probable scenario nailed down now. The last thing we do before he goes to sleep every night is to talk through all the logistics for our upcoming day, so he knows what's coming up tomorrow. It's why we go through exactly what is, and is not, going to happen at an upcoming doctor's appointment, or any new life event that we are heading to. Drew is uncomfortable living with unknowns.

Consider the Israelites and the countless unknowns they faced. As slaves, their lives had been dictated for them and their future looked like more of the same. Generations of Hebrews had lived that way. Now, their future looked completely different. Everything was so unknown, and yet so filled with potential. They lived in a time of incredible excitement and relief (*we are finally free!*), but also with so much uncertainty, they likely lived in an uncomfortable state of being. They didn't know where they were going, who might attack them, or how long they would be wandering without a permanent home. Even the everyday task of eating food looked different than the Slavery Stew to which they were accustomed. Despite Moses' and Aaron's repeated explanations that bread and meat were coming from heaven, and that it would provide the nourishment they needed, when the manna came down, the Israelites were baffled.

> The people are to go out each day and gather enough for that day. In this way I will test them and see whether they will follow my instructions.
>
> That evening quail came and covered the

camp, and in the morning there was a layer of dew around the camp. When the dew was gone, thin flakes like frost on the ground appeared on the desert floor. When the Israelites saw it, they said to each other, "What is it?" For they did not know what it was.

Moses said to them, "It is the bread the Lord has given you to eat..."

The Israelites did as they were told. Some gathered much; some little.[1]

The addition of the dew layer covering the food makes it all so dramatic, doesn't it? God set it up as a big reveal. I envision the dew slowly rising up as it evaporated to reveal the main course, much like you see in the movies or on Food Network when waiters remove lids from plates with great flair. And after the suspense? What was revealed under the giant lid of dew? Frosted flakes. It didn't look like bread or meat at all. The Israelites were rightfully confused.

The word "manna" literally means "What is it?" Moses could have channeled his inner Abbott and Costello at this first reveal. *The dew evaporates. The Hebrews see the white wafers on the ground. They look at the wafer, and then back at Moses. They ask, "Manna?" as in, "What is it?" Moses smiles and replies, "Yes. Manna." And back and forth they go until he relents and explains, "It is the bread the Lord has given you to eat."* That's probably what I would have done.

What God provided for them was unknown, and obviously, not what they were expecting. What if they

---

1 Exodus 16:4b, 13–17a

hadn't eaten it? What if they had said, *God knows we don't like flaky foods; He couldn't possibly have this for us for breakfast. We're waiting for something else—some clear sign that this is what He wants us to eat.*

My kids do this all the time, especially Drew, Mr. Uncertainty Reduction Theory himself. Every single time I am preparing something new, our conversation goes like this:

> *Mom, what's for dinner?*
> [Mom answers with vague description that makes it sound like a food he already loves.]
> *Have I had it before? Did I like it?*
> Always, *Yes.*
> At which point, he distrusts me completely, and he comes to look for himself. And, always, *What is that? I'm not eating that. Gross. I don't like it.*

In Drew's mind, unknown = scary = gross. *If I don't know about it yet, there's no way I will like it and there is no way I want it to be part of my life.*

Why do we live in such fear of the unknown? Okay, I recognize that not everyone does. I should acknowledge up front that Drew has the genetic makeup to be a bit of a scaredy cat when it comes to having fear of an unknown future. (Is it an insult to your child if you blame it on your own genes? I'm not sure.) So I am speaking from a predisposition to hesitate. Some people seek out the unknown, eager to tackle new adventures, embracing the mystery that lies before them. And certainly, the Hebrews had to have a bit of this adventurous spirit within them. As silly as it sounds, the Hebrews needed to muster up the courage for the exodus from slavery. The outcome of that defiant act was a huge unknown, and yet, they began step by step to choose to follow their God and Moses, and walk away from Pharaoh.

For those hesitant to embrace the adventure, sometimes we feel courageous initially until we encounter the first adversity that reminds us we are in unchartered territory. As we follow God to new adventures, the journey is exciting until the obstacles arise. Then suddenly, we start to call everything into question. The Hebrews trucked along away from the Egyptian army until the Red Sea became an issue. Once they overcame that, they realized, no one had packed the stew meat. *Great. Now what are we going to eat? This trip is too much work. Let's go back to what we know.*

Sometimes, the obstacles we face aren't anything more than our own expectations of what we thought the journey would be like. *This looks different than I expected; therefore it must not be good.* Under the Uncertainty Reduction Theory, we reduce discomfort essentially by creating expectations. We gain information about someone to understand them better in order to predict how they will act in the future.

Expectations help us feel more in control. They help us feel like we know what's coming and therefore have less uncertainty about the future. And while it works great for me to explain to Drew what will happen in a routine doctor's appointment, it can be disastrous if I create false expectations for him and they are not

41

met. If he expects that he will not have to get a shot, and he ends up getting one, the unmet expectation of not getting the shot is more detrimental than the fear that he might have had to get one.

Expectations can become mandates if held too tightly. They can become the only way that feels right, because they have created the only way we think we are prepared for. And we risk missing out on unknown but life-changing adventures because we are afraid, or assume that new is bad, or question the journey when it doesn't look like we expected it would.

While fear and preparation have their purpose in keeping us from danger, sometimes unexpected things are unexpected for a reason. I have found that I want my journeys to be adventurous, yet safe. Hair-raising, yet predictable. Full of breath-taking vistas, but not too steep of climbs. Life doesn't often work like that. God doesn't often work like that.

Moses was closer to God than any other wanderer, and he had a deeper understanding of the purpose of the Israelites' journey than anyone else. At the end of it all, as he was sending the new generation of Hebrews across the Jordan, Moses offered this explanation of the journey: "He humbled you, causing you to hunger and then feeding you with manna, *which neither you nor your ancestors had known*, to teach you that man does not live on bread alone but on every word that comes from the mouth of the Lord" (emphasis added).[2]

God brought the Hebrews into the wilderness so that they would feel bewildered. The Hebrews were unable to depend on what they had known. This manna

---

2 Deuteronomy 8:3

was something entirely new; this way of being provided for and being filled up was entirely different from what they had ever experienced before. Their ancestors had no stories to share that made gathering manna feel like a natural, comfortable human way to live. It was God-driven and miraculous. There was no way to exceed or fail to meet expectations, because no one could have expected it.

The Hebrews were on a journey to learn to depend on God, and they still had progress to make. Did you notice who they asked when they didn't know what the manna was? Each other. They did not reach out to the One who had provided the manna.

Uncertainty Reduction Theory posits that people interact when they are motivated to reduce uncertainty. For instance, an individual will likely be more invested in reducing uncertainty if a particular relationship has a lasting presence in his or her life. It's why someone may make an effort to get to know a co-worker with whom they will work daily, but would not be motivated to strike up a conversation in an elevator with someone they may never see again. They invest in reducing uncertainty because they value the relationship in their life. Could it be that God brings us to unknown and maybe discontenting places so that we are motivated to communicate with Him in order to reduce our uncertainty? To help us learn the value of our relationship with Him and to understand His everlasting presence in our lives? Through hunger and the provision of manna, God taught the Hebrews to value their relationship with Him in a new way. Sure, He provided their "bread." But the greater provision was the continual reminder of His daily presence in their lives. Depending on God for bread alone was not enough. Their wholly-dependent relationship on God offered so much more.

THE HEBREWS HAD A CHOICE TO MAKE. They could accept the unknown, knowing God had provided it, trusting that He knew what was best for them, and go about gathering their enough of this new thing called manna. Or they could have chosen not to eat manna, and attempted to find food their own way. They did not control their circumstances, but they did control their response.

So, how did the Israelites respond? Verse 17 tells us, "The Israelites did as they were told." I know they are adults, and it should not warm my heart nearly as much as it does since they are not my children, but can I just park on that phrase for a minute? The wandering tribe did as they were told. Oh, what sweet bliss would exist if those words were ever spoken in our home. I would use half the amount of words I do in a day if my little tribe would simply do as they were told. Or, if I never cooked anything new. Then I wouldn't have to justify so much to Drew before every meal. But, I digress. **God used the unexpected, even in the everyday act of eating, to show the Israelites what they could expect of Him: trustworthiness and goodness.**

And the Israelites stepped out in obedience, once again, into the unknown, and started to gather the Enough that God had provided them.

Unknown Futures and Unexpected Gifts

THERE IS A PARTICULARLY CHEERFUL PARKING VALET at the cancer center of one of our local hospitals. His gait gives him away; he has the step of a man who wants to help. He greets people with a smile, encouraging word or quick-witted quip, and communicates care through his eyes. He learns each patient's treatment schedule so he can have their car parked in front of the door just as they are done—what a profound way to love. He is simply perfect for his job.

The fact that he is a perfect fit for that particular job wasn't always obvious to him. In full disclosure, even though my perception is accurate, my bias is enormous. This parking valet is my dad. Dad worked for years as a rural mail carrier. He was great at that job too, using his gifts to lift others' spirits as he delivered packages on his mail route. But over time, the tendons in his arms became permanently damaged from the repetitive motions of grasping mail, awkwardly steering from the passenger seat, and reaching to the mailbox to deposit mail. Medical treatment helped, but three years from retirement age, he could not continue to deliver the mail and needed to find different work.

Dad fell into a funk. He generally enjoyed the days on his mail route and had no plans to change careers. Suddenly what had once seemed like a secure and comfortable future looked unpredictable and bleak. Being a parking valet was not what he had planned for these years of his life. The parking valet job is a sought-after position for those in retirement; even still, finding alternative, lower paying work just a few years away from a full pension was a harder pill for him to swallow.

At first his new job was very tiring. Mom bought him a step tracker, which revealed that he was walking over seven miles a day between the parking lot and the building as he parked and picked up cars. He hadn't expected that. Even though his arms precluded him from doing his job at the post office, his strong legs became stronger and served him well as a valet. Initially he struggled to find purpose and value in his role—*anybody can park a car,* he thought. (For the record, he knows his daughter cannot, so I take offense at that assumption.) That aside, God did not call him to that job because of his enviable parking skills. Getting to be the first, last, and perhaps only point of encouragement in what is often a stressful and tiring treatment day for a cancer patient isn't what he expected either. That is not something just anyone can do. God has a plan for Dad's unexpected career change, and countless people, including my dad, are being blessed by that plan.

TAKE A MOMENT TO CONSIDER that you have been created, in every single way, for the life that God has planned for you. The path God leads you down may not be the one you expected, but it is the one God has known you would take since before you were created, and it is the one He has uniquely created you to journey. Even those times that were scary, where the future was unknown or you couldn't see the road. Even those times where it seems like you got side-tracked and wasted time wandering like the Hebrews in the desert. All of those paths, those off-shoots, those misadventures, have been valuable in getting you to the place you are today. They are part of your journey, and because of that, part of who you are and how you glorify God.

The daily manna Trust Fall brings to my mind's eye James 1:17, which says, "Every good and perfect gift is from above, coming down from the father of the heavenly lights, who does not change like shifting shadows." Every single good and perfect gift is from above.

Now, this is an easy verse to slap on a birth announcement; it's much harder to proclaim upon the death of a dream. Keep after God about it; ask Him to show you the eternal in the death of your dream. You may be right at the beginning of an exodus toward a Promised Land that you didn't even know existed. Or, you may have some heart-work that is best learned through the hard work of a trial. Those are less fun, but not less rewarding. Hard battles are often the most meaningful victories.

Bear in mind that the Hebrews were not learning to depend on the manna. They were learning to trust the Manna Provider. If the only evidence of God's goodness is us getting what we think we want, we will live a life of disappointment and discontentment. We will be perpetually missing the point. Satan would love for the manna to be the focus. Not only in the amount, which we will talk about in the next chapter, but in all of its characteristics. *Why can't it be stew meat? Why do I have to go gather it; can't it just fall in my bowl?*

The Hebrews journeyed to learn to let God answer their question: *Manna?* A significant lesson in our search for contentment is to let God answer the question: *Manna? What is it?* for us as well. What is our enough? Satan urges us to answer that question by ourselves through creating and holding tightly to our expectations, comparing our circumstances and gifts, and avoiding our fears at all costs. Satan loves it when these things mandate how we spend our days. If we do not look to the Manna Provider to show us the matter of a day in its day, we risk operating from our expectations and fears and missing out on what He has for us. Moments to love others when no one else will, moments to show grace to a child who has screwed up, moments to allow others to take priority over a busy schedule, moments to step out in faith away from comfort zones. Moments to learn life-changing things about ourselves and our God that we never would have expected.

TAKE A LOOK at the last phrase of James 1:17—"the father...who does not change like shifting shadows." God will have experiences for you, struggles, challenges, that you will not expect. He may take you down paths that seem scary; He may "change" course from where you expected to go. But—this is important—He will not change. You can expect Him to be there. When He says He will provide manna daily, you can trust that the manna will be there. If that's His promise, you will be dining on quail in the evening and bread in the morning, Friend. Life may take unexpected turns, but you can know that God expected it, and He will be faithful all the time.

48

God is not one to do the expected. He has a purpose for keeping us on our toes. Take, for instance, the parallel stories of Sarah and Elizabeth in the Bible. Both were older women who had been promised offspring but had surpassed child-bearing years. By a while. That they would be expecting in their old age was certainly...unexpected.

In both cases, the Lord blessed in the same way—the gift of a child. But the responses were remarkably different. When faced with a blessing (that may even be disguised as a trial), we too have the choice to respond with gratitude and thanksgiving like Elizabeth, or with skepticism as Sarah did.

When Sarah learned that God was going to bless her and Abraham with a child, she laughed and thought to herself, "After I am worn out and my lord is old, will I now have this pleasure?"[1] (I told you they were all sarcastic.)

Contrast this with Elizabeth's reaction. Even though her husband Zechariah described his wife as "well along in years" (to my husband, Geoff, I dare you), Elizabeth had a different perspective: "The Lord has done this for me. In these days He has shown His favor and taken away my disgrace among the people."[2]

EVERY DAY WE FACE UNKNOWN FUTURES. We may think we know what to expect, but lives always change in moments—sometimes in one monumental moment, and other times, little by little moments over a period of time. We never truly know what the next day will

---

1 Genesis 18:12
2 Luke 1:25

49

bring. But we do have control over how we respond to what it brings.

It's winter as I write this. A few weeks ago, the forecast called for two to four inches of snow. People in the Midwest are used to living with snow, so when the flurries started flying that Friday morning we went about our business, expecting the snow to stop shortly. These people included my grandpa Helmer at 91 ½ (kids always add the ½ year distinction) and his 93-year-old sister Hazel. They live together and on most days, you can expect them to drive the seventeen miles to the Canton Senior Center to enjoy their noon meal among friends, as they did on this particular day. The expected snowfall amounts, however, fell short of reality. In a few short hours, we received seventeen inches! Grandpa and Hazel were able to make it back home from the Senior Center, but because of all the snow, Grandpa could not drive his car up the long driveway to his acreage. Not to worry. A farmer to the core, Grandpa backed the car into a field driveway across the road and trudged up the driveway to get his tractor. He managed through the snow up the hill and came to retrieve Hazel with his tractor. Hazel does not get around like she used to, having suffered a broken ankle several years prior, and of course, having lived 93 years. Despite trying, Grandpa was not able to hoist Hazel, a solid Norwegian woman, into the cab of the tractor to bring her up the driveway. Not to worry. The tractor had a bucket loader on the front. These two resourceful farm kids situated Hazel standing up in the loader, with her hands securely holding on to the back as Grandpa Helmer drove her up the driveway and safely back to their home. I giggle every time I think of it.

Grandpa Helmer and Hazel did not control the weather, but they did control the way they responded to the weather. And no, Hazel's ride up the driveway was likely not what she expected; she might have even had some fear about it. But, she faced the fear head on (well, technically backside first), but ended up having a ride of a lifetime and a great story to tell!

MY DAD EXPECTED TO WORK for the post office until he retired. He wanted to do that. But his medical condition created a situation beyond his control that challenged his expectation. He struggled. But then do you know what he did? He persevered. He showed up day after day and chose to bless others with his gift of encouragement. Dad did not control his circumstances and those circumstances did not meet his expectations, but he could control his response to those unmet expectations. Controlling our response to circumstance, especially an ongoing, life-altering change of circumstances, is not a one-time success. We must choose to respond in obedience and trust over and over again. Every single day, except the seventh, week after week, the Hebrews needed to choose to go out and gather enough. That was all they got. The daily act of obedience taught dependence. It allowed them to see that God was consistently faithful in providing their Enough for that day.

contentment

"Each one gathered as much as he needed."

ONCE THE ISRAELITES BECAME COMFORTABLE with their food falling from the sky, they set about a daily harvest routine. Each day they set out to gather as much as they needed. Did you notice that the Israelites didn't all gather the same amount of manna, but when it was measured, no one had too much and no one had too little? In case you missed it, here it is again:

> Moses also said, "You will know that it was the Lord when He gives you meat to eat in the evening and all the bread you want in the morning, because He has heard your grumbling against Him. Who are we? You are not grumbling against us, but against the Lord."
> The Lord said to Moses, "I have heard the grumbling of the Israelites. Tell them, 'At

twilight you will eat meat, and in the morning you will be filled with bread. Then you will
know that I am the Lord your God.'"

That evening quail came and covered the
camp, and in the morning there was a layer
of dew around the camp. When the dew was
gone, thin flakes like frost on the ground appeared on the desert floor. When the Israelites saw it, they said to each other, "What is
it?" For they did not know what it was.

Moses said to them, "It is the bread the
Lord has given you to eat. This is what the
Lord has commanded: 'Each one is to gather
as much as he needs.' Take an omer for each
person you have in your tent."

The Israelites did as they were told; some
gathered much, some little. And when they
measured it...he who gathered much did not
have too much, and he who gathered little did
not have too little. Each one gathered as much
as he needed.[1]

Each one is to gather as much as he needs. God
does not have a limited supply of blessing and provision. He's not going to run out of the good stuff. We
don't need to worry that if someone else has been
blessed, there isn't enough to go around for us. God
has **enough** for all of us. And how much is that? Early in
the passage when Moses explains manna to the Israel-

---

1 Exodus 16:8, 11–18. Also, for those of you wondering what an omer is,
verse 36 tells us: "(An omer is one tenth of an ephah.)" Glad I could clear
that up for you.

ites for the first time, he explains that "You will know that it was the Lord when He gives you meat to eat in the evening and *all the bread you want* in the morning" (emphasis added). But when the Lord again explains this to Moses, He clarifies, "Tell them, 'At twilight you will eat meat, and in the morning you will be *filled with bread.* Then you will know that I am the Lord your God." God's measure was different than Moses'. God does not measure based on our external wants; God measures based on what will fulfill our internal needs.

The Israelites had differing circumstances from one another. At the simplest level, some had more people in their tent than others, and therefore needed more manna than others. That makes sense. But when I read, "some gathered much, some little," I can't help but wonder: Do you think the Hebrews compared with one another? Do you think they brought their baskets of manna to the measuring station and noticed the difference? Perhaps some man made a passive aggressive joke to another about the number of kids he must have had in his tent; "Looks like you've got enough there to feed Pharaoh's army!" (and then his wife firmly nudged him and mouthed "Too soon.") Despite God providing all the manna they needed, I cannot help but wonder if the human tendency to compare reared its ugly head.

Oh, how Satan loves it when we compare our circumstances with the circumstances of others! He loves to disguise comparison as the more objective-sounding notion of fairness. He wants us to believe that we can objectively look at our situation, the situation of another, and evaluate the two rationally and with full understanding. He invites us, prods us, taunts us to ascend the steps to the throne of Judgment, to boldly plop down, and to righteously make a declaration that all is, or is not, right with the world. But the truth is this: Determining fairness is not an objective activity; "fair" requires that we compare.

Satan loves comparison as a buzz-kill so much for that reason; it creates a distorted reality for both parties. For the party that comes up lacking, comparison can lead to jealousy, anger, bitterness, and self-doubt. For the party who wins, it can lead to contempt, pride, and false confidence. I'm not seeing a lot of fruits of the spirit in the comparison results line-up. Satan's greatest purpose is to pull us off our game in order to thwart us from fulfilling our God-given purposes. One of his best tactics is to confuse us as to what that purpose is, and one of his favorite methods for doing that is to suggest that perhaps what others are doing is what we should be doing. Or what others have is what we should have. He can be very conniving, often aligning our vantage point ever-so-subtly so that others' lives or work appear more rewarding, more fulfilling, more purposeful, more important, more glamourous. Anything he can do to make it seem that what we have or what we are doing is not enough. When he succeeds, we either turn our focus to striving toward what we think we want to have or do, or we stop the doing altogether, having lost our sense of God-given value. Over time, Satan's salami-slicing shaves away at our contentment and slowly but persistently pulls us away from our created purpose, ultimately trying to pull the Created away from our Creator.

When we are looking at others and what they are doing, or how they are living, or what they have, or what we do not have, we stop looking to God for our matter of the day in its day—for our Enough. God would not have us look at our life circumstances in comparison to what He has given, or not given, others. In Galatians 6:4, Paul writes, "Each one should test their own actions. Then they can take pride in themselves alone, without comparing themselves to someone else, for each one should carry their own load."

We have each been created for different purposes on this Earth. God has given us particular tools, resources, trials, circumstances, relationships, and gifts in order to fulfill those purposes. Satan knows that and doesn't like it. He wants us looking at others rather than God to see how we stack up. He wants us to be paralyzed by distraction, or better yet, bitterness. Notice that in the amount of manna God provided to the Israelites, they each had what they needed. God promised that if the Israelites gathered what they needed, they would be "filled with bread." **God doesn't promise fairness. God promises fullness.**

Our three boys are relatively close in age with less than four years difference between the oldest and the youngest. They play really well together. And they play really horribly together as well. It seems that any two of them can play together well, and it doesn't particularly matter which two it is. But, when the third one enters the picture, they begin to jockey for position. There's just something about that third wheel when it comes to relationships that turns things all off-kilter, isn't there? The Three-in-One is the perfect design for the Trinity, but in our house a three-stranded cord will not only not be quickly broken, it will likely be used to try to strangle someone.

On certain days, the boys compare and contend over everything. Every. Thing. Some days, I reach the end of my three-stranded rope. On one of these days, I decided to address the constant one-upping of each other on a level they would understand—the pee and poop level. This is where we live in most conversations these days anyway. So, I explained to them the concept of the peeing contest and how it's used to describe people trying to prove to be better than someone else. *Can't we all giggle at what a silly contest that would be*, I continued. Surely, they could see my point and we could all walk away having learned a valuable lesson about the silliness of comparing ourselves to others. Giggle, giggle. Lesson learned. Turns out they learned something different than what I had intended. Later that evening, Drew came running excitedly down the stairs exclaiming that he had won and that I should come and see! As I followed him back up the stairs to the site of the contest, I naively wondered what contest he had won, excited for him that he had won something against his older brothers. That's when I saw Jake and Ben standing in the bathroom, excitedly reliving the contest: "He hit carpet!" Drew won two contests that day. One against his brothers, and one against his mother. But let's be real: No one really wins in a peeing contest.

The comparison issue is directly tied to the contentment issue. When we are discontent with who we are, we start to compare. The thing is, the world has a lot of people in it. With lots of different circumstances.

And if we look hard enough, we will find someone with part of a situation that looks better than what we have. The thief who comes to kill, steal, and destroy would love to help point that out to us. Anything he can do to take our eyes off the One on whom we can depend.

If contentment can only be found in knowing that *compared to someone else* you have what you want and need, the measurement is always changing. Under that measure, contentment always depends on who is standing beside you. And how you stack up compared to them (based, of course, on the measure you choose). As that person, or that element of comparison changes, so does your level of contentment. If you find yourself having "less," the desire to strive increases. The exhausting cycle continues.

Comparison often leads to us wanting more. The passion for "more" in and of itself is not bad. God wants more for us too. Jesus came so that we might have life and have it abundantly. I'm not talking prosperity gospel here. I'm talking, and more importantly He's talking, about a life that matters. A life with purpose. But that life is not based on what He's giving to others. As we look to Him, instead of looking sideways, day-by-day, He reveals what that life is for us. If we look to what others are getting, we become less of who we were created to be. And less content.

But hear this from 1 Timothy 6:6—"Godliness with contentment is great gain." Or, as it so perfectly says in the Message,

> "A devout life does bring wealth, but it's the rich simplicity of being yourself before God.

Since we entered the world penniless and will
leave it penniless, if we have bread on the table and shoes on our feet, that's enough."

Enough: the rich simplicity of being yourself before God.
I cannot think of any better description of contentment
than that.

Our life will never be full if we try to fill it up apart
from God. He desired for the Israelites to be filled with
manna, so that they would know that He is the Lord.
In the same way, He provides the matter of the day in
its day for us so we might better know Him, too. If "it"
doesn't come, then we don't need it. Fairness, defined
as "someone else has it," does not equal fullness. Some
may gather much, and some may gather little. But if
we look to God to provide what we need, each one will
gather and be filled with exactly as much as he needs.

Quit Comparing

WE SPEND MANY SUMMER WEEKENDS at a lake cabin near the resort area of Okoboji, Iowa. One weekend several years ago, I was pushing Drew in a stroller around Gull Point State Park, a nature reserve near the cabin. Quite a few other people were on the same path, enjoying the scenic water views, gorgeous oak trees, and other relaxing sights of nature. I, on the other hand, was racing them. I began to notice how many people I was passing on my walk. Sheepishly, I will tell you that I started to congratulate myself on how quick I was, or more accurately, how much quicker I was than everyone else. Everyone else, that is, enjoying their stroll, completely unaware that they had entered into a competitive walking competition. Good grief.

Just then, fast-paced footsteps interrupted the cheering section in my head. As the footsteps drew closer, I knew they were threatening to overtake my lead. Immediately, I started listing all the excuses as to why I couldn't be expected to maintain my lead. In fact, these excuses were the same reasons that I was so proud of myself just seconds earlier. *I was pushing a stroller after all, and it's hard for young mothers to find time to exercise.* The footsteps were getting closer. I started to turn to say "good morning" to my pursuer, and to perhaps remind him or her that it was a nice morning for a *casual* stroll, wasn't it?

I turned my head, and that's when I saw it. Belly. By my estimation, about eight months of it. An extremely pregnant woman was leaving me in the dust! I laughed at God's perfectly-timed and humorously-communicated message to me: Get over yourself and your silly pride, and let go of your excuses. This path of life you are on—this race—is about you and Me, and no one else.

Our quest to regain the contentment that Satan continually works to salami-slice away will never be won until we learn to look up to be filled up. Looking sideways will only show us how much manna someone else has in her basket. That basket is not my basket. And the basket next to you is not your basket either, Friend. What's in her basket is not the enough God has for you and for your basket. There's enough out there for everyone, but that manna is not yours. Let her gather her manna, and you gather yours.

This is not to say that God doesn't ever want us looking sideways; certainly this life is meant to be about more than simply us. We journey as a tribe, whether that tribe is close friendships, family relationships, church communities, or all of the above, and God has purpose in this arrangement. Raising children may take a village, but living life to the full takes a tribe. We do not go out and gather alone. We are gathering enough, side by side. But, as we look to those around us, the purpose and object of our gaze matters greatly. Satan would have you look sideways at another's basket to compare. God would have you look at people in order to connect with and encourage them.

I HAVE TWO STORIES TO SHARE about the purpose of our tribes, one where I got it wrong, and one where someone else got it right.

Last Fourth of July, my family and I sat around our dinner table after our weekend guests had left, all of us tired from a fun, activity-filled weekend. Earlier in the day, we had enjoyed one of our favorite Fourth of July traditions—the slip and slide. This is not your typical slip and slide. Think bigger. Think 100 feet of heavy-duty plastic sheeting staked to the ground, drizzled with no-tears baby shampoo (no tears is an important, hard-learned detail), soaked with a garden hose at the top and a sprinkler half way down, sloped down the giant hill in our backyard. It's a huge hit! Sometimes, we even let the kids have a turn.

We sat eating reheated hot dogs and hamburgers from a picnic potluck several days before. One of the boys squirted ketchup onto his plate and a small bit missed the plate and landed on the table. He quickly swiped it up with his finger and licked off the evidence. His older brother was appalled at his grossness (read: overtired and looking for a fight); he laid into the younger one in ironic disgust. I, being equally tired and cranky, decided to teach the older one a lesson.

"You don't think you've done anything gross today?" I questioned. He didn't think he had. I offered back to him the story he had told me right before dinner of how he had taken a straw to drink the melted ice that remained in the drink cooler from the weekend. I asked whether he thought drinking water countless people had stuck their hands in all weekend was gross.

The accuser seemed to accept my point and got quiet. We both thought the point had been made. Geoff, who had been listening, had not heard the water-drinking story originally and seemed extremely grossed out by it when I shared it. His eyes got big and he said, "He didn't actually do that, did he?" My son and I, both slightly confused, nodded that he had (not sure why Geoff was *that* grossed out by it). And then, Geoff's reason became clear: "I soaked my feet in that water earlier today!"

All this grossness aside, I was wrong to try to prove my son acted grosser than his brother (although I'm fine with the secondary lesson of knowing where your drinking water has been before you drink it). I had missed the point and had encouraged comparison rather than connection. I had an opportunity to demonstrate kindness in order to teach kindness, and instead I went with "yeah, but you're grosser." Moms can be so human sometimes.

In hindsight, I wished I had let it go and not said a thing. I wished I had modeled, through restraint, that God created families, communities, churches, friendships—whatever relationship it may be—to build each other up and spur each other on, not to tear down. God did not create Eve so that Adam would have an opponent, or a benchmark from which to compare himself. He created her for his companionship and love.

Tribe life can be hard. Especially when we are tired. But there is beautiful purpose in our togetherness as it teaches us to love those who are up in our business. "Love your neighbor as yourself" is not an easy commandment. God knows that; He knows it takes patience and practice that must be developed over time. Perhaps it's why He gave us siblings.

So I BOTCHED IT THAT DAY, but I wake up and try again tomorrow, thankful I am still among the tribe. And I am so thankful that my tribe includes friends who get it right. Way, way, way back when I was in high school, I had a great smile. In fact, I had the Best Smile. At least, that's what my classmates declared in the senior class vote. (I was also up for Most Musical, so take the declaration with a large grain of salt.) The results of the survey were included in the West Lyon Community School yearbook, along with a picture of each winner. There was only one slight problem. On the day the yearbook staff needed to take the picture of my Best Smile, I had just returned from the dentist, having had a cavity filled. Half of my face was completely numb! When I tried to smile, I looked like a "winner," indeed. My saving grace, however, was my friend Lance Wulf. He had won Best Smile for the boys and was going to be in the picture with me. He took one look at my smile, and decided that it would be funny for us both to offer lopsided smiles for the camera. His smile might have looked weirder than mine! What an awesome friend.

You know who else did this well? Jesus (big shocker there). He was willing to get into the thick of it with His friends. One night, Jesus retreated to pray and sent the disciples on ahead in a boat. It says in Mark 6:48 that in the middle of that night, "He saw the disciples straining at the oars, because the wind was against them." He walked on the water to them, which is cool, but what He does next is my favorite: "Then He climbed into the boat with them, and the wind died down." I love that He didn't calm the storm from the shore. He didn't walk out beside them and say "watch this." He climbed into the boat with them. He met His friends where they were.

Sometimes we need to get ugly with those we care about. We need to be willing to be vulnerable and authentic. We are not perfect like Jesus, but showing our imperfections may be exactly what our friends need to see. I am so encouraged by my friends when they keep it real with me. The Best Smiles come off, and we share our struggles, our missteps, our failures. I know that as a mom, in particular, I have often compared myself with moms who appear to be able to walk on water. From a distance, they appear to have it altogether (which, on certain days in my world, may just mean her kids are all wearing shoes). Many of these other mothers are my friends. And because they are who they are, they do not let me keep my perception of their perfection. They reveal their lopsided Best Smiles to me. They get in the boat with me. They strain with me. We are ugly together, and it is a most beautiful picture of Christ-like friendship.

We are not Jesus. We cannot walk on water. We cannot say the word and calm the wind for our friends. But we can make a difference. We can show up and do real life with our friends—not being afraid to close the distance and be there for someone in need. Like Jesus did for His friends.

Women, this comparison issue is often a tough one for us. The effects of comparing ourselves to others can run the gamut from low self-esteem and mostly internally focused, to downright catty and externally toxic to all those around. We are relational beings, but if we're not careful, the desire to be relational turns into the reality of being all-about-the-business of someone else. We can do better than that. We can reflect Christ's love better than that. Not only to others, but to ourselves as well. Let's free each other up to run our own races.

One more thing: we each have incomparable gifts for a reason. These gifts build up our tribes and our world as a whole. They are not the same as another's, because everyone having the same gifting would be stupid. We need diversity as it makes us unique and as it provides things we would not otherwise have. Take, for instance, the literal gift of gift-giving. There are, in general, what I will call extravagant gift givers and practical gift givers. I am one of the practical gift givers. I am not that popular at baby showers. People tend to ooh and aah much more over the four-piece baby gown complete with petticoat and crinoline (that the baby will never, ever put his or her cute little chubby cheeks in) than they do the thoughtful box of diapers and washcloths that will get used EVERY. SINGLE. DAY. I mean, hypothetically, I imagine, people will be less excited about that.

But we need both the extravagant gift-givers and the diaper and washcloth ones. Both serve a valuable purpose in our tribes. **We have been given different gifts so that we can be different gift givers, both literally but also universally as we use all the gifts we have been given.** These unique attributes make up the core of who we truly are, which is different from who other people are. Rather than compare what others are or are not against what we are or are not, we should celebrate those different gifts, and be both extravagant and practical stewards of them.

SHORTLY BEFORE JESUS' DEATH, Judas, the disciple who betrayed Jesus, witnessed a woman named Mary anoint Jesus' feet with her expensive perfume and wash His feet with her hair. Mary had been gifted with a heart that loved her Lord extravagantly, but Judas questioned why she hadn't used the perfume in a more practical manner, like selling it and giving the money to the poor. Jesus responded, as told in Mark 14:6-8.

> Leave her alone. Why are you bothering her? She has done a beautiful thing to me. The poor you will always have with you, and you can help them any time you want. But you will not always have me. She did what she could. She poured perfume on my body beforehand to prepare for my burial.

She used her gift to serve Jesus. *She did what she could.* When it seems like we have such little to offer or the world would tell us that we are not offering our gifts the way in which we should be, remember that Jesus does not see it the same way. Be who you are. Do what you can. And hear Jesus' response to you as you pour yourself out in service to Him and to others: "She has done a beautiful thing to me." Now that's something to ooh and aah about.

If we use our gifts like that, we become a stronger

tribe. Take it one step further and do what Jesus did: rather than compare, acknowledge the gifts of others as beautiful and recognize their efforts. Be part of a tribe that looks sideways in order to build each other up, not tear each other down.

a holy Sabbath

"Nevertheless"

LIFE GETS PRETTY HECTIC for our family sometimes. My hard-working husband works a wild schedule as an accountant, which probably goes without saying since being a CPA is pretty much synonymous with wild living. Our four kids are not over-involved in activities (yet), but one or two things for each every week fills up our time quickly. Both Geoff and I are involved in various ways at church and school as well as with bible studies and church life group, and as is the case for many others, nearly every week feels full. Generally, our time is spent in good ways (I'm totally ignoring my Facebook addiction as I write that), but busy isn't always better.

Sometimes during these weeks, I think longingly back to my hospital stays after each child was born. Is that weird? All four of our deliveries were C-sections, so it seems rather odd that I remember post-surgery recovery so fondly. Obviously, I was happily medicated.

And certainly, a huge part of that rose-colored memory is the new baby I snuggled as I memorized its precious face. But what I look back so fondly on, and what I long so much for, is that short period of time I was able to stop and focus on one thing. All I had to do during that time in the hospital was recover and love on my new baby. No striving, no running—just being. I knew what I was to be doing and I could focus on what mattered in that moment.

God recognizes the importance of having time to be still, of allowing one's self the breathing room to say: "Enough doing; it's time to rest." He modeled this for us by resting after six days of creation, and He offered the same respite to the Israelites in the form of a day of rest, a holy Sabbath to the Lord.

> Each morning everyone gathered as much as he needed, and when the sun grew hot, it melted away. On the sixth day, they gathered twice as much—two omers for each person—and the leaders of the community came and reported this to Moses. He said to them, "This is what the Lord commanded: 'Tomorrow is to be a day of rest, a holy Sabbath to the Lord. So bake what you want to bake and boil what you want to boil. Save whatever is left and keep it until morning.'"
>
> So they saved it until morning, as Moses commanded, and it did not stink or get maggots in it. "Eat it today," Moses said, "because today is a Sabbath to the Lord. You will not find any of it on the ground today. Six days you

are to gather it, but on the seventh day, the Sabbath, there will not be any."

Nevertheless, some of the people went out on the seventh day to gather it, but they found none. Then the Lord said to Moses, "How long will you refuse to keep my commands and my instructions? Bear in mind that the Lord has given you the Sabbath; that is why on the sixth day He gives you bread for two days. Everyone is to stay where He is on the seventh day; no one is to go out." So the people rested on the seventh day.[1]

Recall the story of Pharaoh's demands in Exodus 5; he required them to work for "the matter of the day in its day," but took away the straw that he had been providing. He demanded more from them, but provided less. In a way, God also demanded more by doubling their recommended daily allowance of manna on the sixth day. The first time He explained manna to Moses, He simply told them they would gather twice as much without explaining the payoff: "On the sixth day they are to prepare what they bring in, and that is to be twice as much as they gather on the other days."[2] The difference between the two though, is that God blessed that extra effort by providing more—not only more manna, but more quality of life. He intended the next day to be set aside so the Israelites could be purposeful in worship. To rest in God's sufficient provision.

1 Exodus 16:21–30
2 Exodus 16:5

Nevertheless. Nevertheless, some people went out to harvest on the seventh day. Ever wonder if God gets exasperated? I wonder how often He watches the anxious actions of His people, knowing what He has asked of them, shakes His Holy head, and thinks, "Nevertheless, they strive." Despite all He offered and provided as a gift to His people, nevertheless, people continued to strive after more.

The renegades already had what they needed. It wasn't that the people going out to get more didn't heed the previous instruction to save part of their double portion from the day before. It says, "So they saved it until morning." They had the leftovers boxed up in the fridge ready to eat; they were simply seeking out more.

To be fair, when the Israelites were under Pharaoh's authority, a never-quit work ethic would have been to their benefit; more than that, it was likely life-preserving. Perhaps they thought working harder would impress God. But God had a different way. He wanted more for His people, but not in a way they yet understood. He wanted them to rest in Him. He wanted to provide their Enough, to show them that an abundant life is not about material abundance.

It appears from the telling of the story that they also had what I will call a Toddler Mindset. Notice, the Lord does not call them out for forgetting the instruction. It was not a lack of understanding that brought them out to seek manna on the seventh day. He knew their hearts; they were *refusing* to obey. They were making a choice to do it their own way. Sound anything like any toddlers you know? We have one of those at our house right now, and she is amped up with the same genetic disposition to buck the system that her mom has. Good times.

I don't know why they went out to look for more. Moses had already told them there would not be any. In her book, *Breathe*, Priscilla Shirer suggests that because of their slave history, the Israelites needed to learn a completely new mindset. They had a slave mindset and needed to learn a different type of dependence. She writes:

> Commanding the people to take a Sabbath was Yahweh's way of showing these newly freed people that their relationship with Him was not based on what they could do for Him. He loved them simply because they were His. He had chosen them. That was enough.[3]

Their merit was not based on their ability to work well; their merit was based solely on to whom they belonged. **As God's children, they were enough. They did not need to do more.**

OUR TODDLER DAUGHTER, LILY, is just starting to enjoy having us read books to her. I'm especially excited about this, because before having the desire to read them, all she wanted to do was eat them. The corner edges of nearly all our toddler books would suggest that the Knoblochs have a dog.

---

3 Priscilla Shirer, *Breathe: Making Room for the Sabbath* (Nashville: Lifeway Press, 2014), 49.

One of Lily's favorite books is *God Loves You*.[4] It's not flashy, or overly clever, but it's a keeper. And although it loses a little something without the cute illustrations, these snippets portray the worthwhile message:

> You can be silly or you can be sad.
> You can be merry or you can be mad.
> You can be grumpy or you can be glad.
> God loves you just as you are....
>
> You can be messy or you can be neat.
> You can be poky or fast on your feet.
> March with the others or to your own beat.
> God loves you just as you are....
>
> God made each part from your head to your toe.
> Day in and day out He is helping you grow.
> God made you special and that's how you know
> God loves you just as you are.

Simple but solid, right? What a great message for children to hear over and over (and over) again. I believe every word of that book for my daughter, and for all of my kids. Every single word. I would never want them thinking anything else about their unique qualities and the special design God had in mind when He made them.

So when did it become difficult to believe those words for me? When did my perspective become kitty-wampus (auto correct doesn't like that word, but I do) and I started thinking I needed to strive for something

---

4 Kathleen Long Bostrom and Elena Kucharik, *God Loves You* (Wheaton, IL: Tyndale, 2001).

more than I had already been given as a dearly-loved child of God?

Please soak this in again, Friend: God loves you simply because you are His. He loves the you that He knows; God loves you just as you are.

God loved the Israelites enough to rescue them, just as they were. God loved the Israelites enough to pursue them, even as they continued to turn back to old ways of thinking. We will see this time and time again in the journey of the Hebrews; they were not quick to figure it out, but God was patient. If that's true, and since God never changes, then perhaps there is hope for us. Perhaps when we are not quick to figure out simple messages, like *God loves you just as you are*, He will be faithful in continuing to pursue us and point us back to the truth.

God met the Hebrews at the place they needed instruction: in their minds and in their hearts. His instruction was simple: "Bear in mind that the Lord has given you the Sabbath." He invited them to let live in their mind the truth that this time was a time of rest and that to worship is a gift, a gift given by the Lord. They were not to do "what made sense to them" or "what they had always done" or even "what they saw others doing." All of those lines of thinking were missing the point. God was teaching a new way that required obedience and dependence. And by living in that mindset, the Hebrews could see the Sabbath for the blessing it was. But they had to cease striving first. They would not find it by doing it their way. The "more" they truly wanted would not come from doing more of the same.

Perhaps we too need to learn a new way. Maybe

we're stuck in a slave mindset? We may not be leaving a physical bondage, but could we be in a mental struggle from which we need to be set free? Are there things we need to bear in mind that we are no longer enslaved to? Are we seeking "more" of something that we don't need?

Just as God rescued the Israelites out of slavery and patiently sought to retrain their minds, so too He has rescued us and desires for us to learn a new way. As we keep our eyes on Him and allow Him to order our day, we shake off the shackles that bind and we can live in freedom. It will require some retraining—some bearing in mind. But God is patient, and He is a great teacher. And He has given us a mighty resource in the Holy Spirit. Hear this truth from Galatians 5:1—"It is for freedom that Christ has set us free. Stand firm, then, and do not let yourselves be burdened again by a yoke of slavery." There is a better way.

When Strivings Cease

MY FRIEND ADAM IS A GENIUS. Adam is slightly quirky, as most geniuses are. Exhibit A: Back in the day to convince his now-wife, April, to go on a first date with him, he took the traditional approach and called her on the phone (back when phones were used for calling and not just texting). But being Adam, he didn't just ask her, he commanded her. When April answered, he spoke in his deepest, most serious-sounding voice: "April, this is God. I want you to go on a date with Adam." How does one say no to God? The man is brilliant.

Adam continues to use his superb intelligence in parenting their four children. April, to whom God speaks, shared a story of how she and Adam were trying to get their children to finish the last of the broccoli left from dinner. In an impulsive moment, Adam offered his daughter, Vanessa, 10,000 points if she would finish the broccoli. Who could pass up a deal like that? She gobbled it up, and earned the points. Winner, winner, broccoli dinner. Adam utilized this point technique throughout the evening, and his children racked up the points as they completed various household chores.

Adam's intellect, however, did not stop at his generation. Several times during the evening, his oldest daughter, Savannah, stopped to ask—"Dad, what are the points for?" Father, what are we striving after? It is a worthy question to ask.

How often do we act like Adam's children, chasing after "pointless" things, never stopping to ask as Savannah did, "Father, is what I'm chasing after worth it?" We can so easily get distracted by the enticement that doing more might get us ahead, put us in the lead, make us the winner. Who doesn't want to be the winner? But of what? What have we gained? Do we even know what we are chasing after? If we don't, how do we learn a new way?

GOD DAILY PROVIDED FOR THE HEBREWS with 100% consistency. All throughout the Old Testament, He did miraculous things for His people and yet, they were discontent. They continued to go back to their old ways of thinking—willing to endure slavery for a good cup of stew. How did they miss the daily miracle of God's provision being unveiled right before their eyes? How was it not enough for them? Have you thought that? I know I have. I've even taken it one judgmental step farther and smugly compared myself to them: *If God offered obvious daily miracles like manna in my life, I would never struggle to trust and obey.* (Because I've clearly taken to heart that comparison is unhelpful.) Whether you are with me or not, I am not alone in thinking this way. Generations before us have asked this same question. In fact, Jesus had this same conversation with the crowds in Capernaum who had followed Him there.

> So they asked Him, "What miraculous sign *Chloe*
> then will you give that we may see it and be-

lieve you? What will you do? Our forefathers
ate the manna in the desert; as it is written:
'He gave them bread from heaven to eat.'"[1]

They wanted proof from the Son of God. They
wanted to know He was dependable and trustworthy. I
get it. They didn't want to take Him on His Holy Word
that He was the Messiah. The crowds needed just a little more reassurance that He had the almighty power
necessary to be their Savior.

I should stop here and provide a little context to
this conversation the dubious crowd was having with
Jesus. This conversation took place the day after Jesus
fed the five thousand men, not to mention women and
children, with a measly five loaves of bread and two
fish. I will pause so you can digest the irony. . . .

Did you catch it? These same people asking for
a definite sign of His almighty power were following
Him because of this miracle they had witnessed immediately before. God in the flesh had just provided
bread—of all things!—to a large group of people in a
miraculous fashion. It's, like, the exact same scenario
as God providing manna to their ancestors, and they
missed it. All throughout the New Testament, Jesus
performed these miracles, and yet the people didn't
believe. They thought they needed more.

Here I sit, convicted, as He reveals in my mind all
that has not changed. All throughout time, up to present day, God has been performing miracles right in
front of, and even within, His people, and we are missing them because we are looking for something else. Or

---

1 John 6:30-31

something more. He has provided His Spirit within us, and we think the messages are not quite clear. Do we take Him at His Holy Word either? Jesus' response to them serves as a pretty clear message to us as well:

> It is my Father who gives you the true bread from heaven. For the bread of God is He who comes down from heaven and gives life to the world.[2]
>
> Then Jesus declared, 'I am the bread of life. He who comes to me will never go hungry, and he who believes in me will never be thirsty. But as I told you, you have seen me and still you do not believe me.'[3]
>
> I am the bread of life. Your forefathers ate the manna in the desert, yet they died. But here is the bread that comes down from heaven, which a man may eat and not die. I am the living bread that came down from heaven. If anyone eats of this bread, he will live forever. This bread is my flesh, which I will give for the life of the world.[4]

He even stayed with the manna metaphor, for crying out loud. Jesus is pleading for the Jews to understand that He is manna from heaven—a bread that fills and that offers life. He may not look and act like the Messiah they expected, but He is what they needed. And like them, we don't need more miracles to see that. We

---

2 John 6:32b–33
3 John 6:35–36
4 John 6:48–51

don't need clearer signs to know for sure He's talking to us. Our minds don't need convincing as much as re-training. Jesus came to earth to show us His father. He came to show us that the Father is enough for us.

WE'VE COME TO ANOTHER EXAMPLE of how God speaks "Enough" over our desire for contentment. Early in the book-writing process, I texted a friend to let her know God had given me "Enough" as the direction for the book. She texted in response: "Yes. All we need. When strivings cease." As I started writing, that phrase stuck with me, "When strivings cease." It felt like an "enough" definition worth considering. Perhaps this phrase is most familiar to you, as it was to me, from the lyrics of the well-known hymn, *In Christ Alone*.

> In Christ alone my hope is found,
> He is my light, my strength, my song;
> This Cornerstone, this solid ground,
> Firm through the fiercest drought and storm.
> What heights of love, what depths of peace,
> When fears are stilled, *when strivings cease!*
> My Comforter, my All in All,
> Here in the love of Christ I stand.[5]

I was surprised to learn, however, that the phrase is taken from one of my favorite verses, Psalm 46:10. Perhaps you know the verse, like I do, as: "Be still and know that I am God." But the New American Standard Bible translation reads this way: "Cease striving, and

---

5 Stuart Townend and Keith Getty. *In Christ Alone* (Brentwood: Capitol CMG, 2002).

know that I am God." Unbeknownst to my friend who texted me, she had led me to a very cool connection.

As I studied further, I learned that the original Hebrew phrase for "cease striving" or "be still" translates more directly as a command—"Stop!"—such that the verse would read, "**Enough**! Now know that I am God."[6] How cool is that? Hold this verse close to your heart and consider how God would call you to be still. To cease striving. Take a minute, right now, to consider where He may be firmly speaking "Enough!" over some area of your life. Go ahead, I'll wait.

STOP! Two THINGS. First: I wanted you who had not completed the exercise from the previous paragraph but had just continued reading to think that I had caught you in the act. (I would have been in this group of readers, by the way.) But for the second group, those of you who did consider where God was calling you to be still, that message is for you as well. In what area of your life, or what behaviors or thought patterns or life choices, is He calling you to "STOP!"?

Maybe it's a striving toward something easily seen, materialistic perhaps. You are striving for more money and things. I would venture to guess that money and stuff is not the endgame for many of you though. Perhaps money is the means by which we think we will gain what we're striving after, but at the heart of it, that's not what many of us are after. Our striving is for something more subtle, something more elusive. Security? Acceptance? Validation? Purpose? There is this

---

6 *The NIV Study Bible*, 10th Anniversary Edition (Grand Rapids: Zondervan Publishing House, 1995), 826.

underlying feeling—this gnawing, unsettling, discontented thought that plagues me in the bathtub—that there's more "something" out there, or that there might be, and that I might not be doing enough—for God, for my kids, for my marriage, for my career, for my parents, for my church, for my community, for my school—to get it.

We will never achieve "it" on our own. The truth is: "it" does not exist on this Earth.

THIS STRIVING—THIS ANXIOUS STRIVING—leaves us feeling inadequate and insufficient because each of us is striving to be our own god. We are striving to know and feel, based on our own abilities, secure, accepted, validated, purposeful. To be independently important. Security, acceptance, validation, purpose are all things God wants for you, and for me. If we are seeking them apart from God, we are striving in the wrong direction to receive them. Our Creator created us to depend upon Him to find Enough. To feel secure, accepted, validated, and purposeful, because we are children of God. The bread of life—Jesus—the living bread came down from heaven so that we might have life to the full. **Seeking after things that require less of Him is striving to be something less than we were created to be. And so He calls out to us:** *STOP!* Like a parent yelling to a child about to cross the street, God urges us to STOP!; let Him hold our hand.

Several years ago, Geoff and I were determined to make it to church on time. We had two kids at the time, and the feat seemed really hard. As I frantically struggled to dress Jacob, who was one at the time, the

effort looked more like a game of Twister than me simply putting a shirt on a child. In desperation I thought,
*Lord, make me an octopus so I have enough arms to handle
this child!* He didn't. Rather, in His infinite wisdom He
chose to calm Jacob down long enough for me to finish
getting his clothes on. In hindsight, that would have
been a better thing to ask for.

How often I think I know what I need, and so I set
about going to get it. By myself. If I just work a little
harder, gather a few more resources. (More arms, perhaps...really, Elise? An octopus? Who prays for that?)
Now, by no means am I saying that in a more rational
moment, I would have thought that actually becoming
an octopus would have been the best solution to my
problem at hand, but that simply illustrates another
point: we can be very inefficient strivers.

In the heat of the moment, we are not always
thinking clearly. Our minds are so limited by our perception of time, our limited understanding of the circumstances in which we find ourselves, and our narrow
focus on our immediate surroundings, that left to our
own devices, we can reach some horribly misguided
conclusions as to what we need.

But God hears us even if we grumble, as the Hebrews did; He still provides. The God of the universe
knows my true desires. He doesn't get distracted by
what I say, but knows at the core what I mean, and what
I need. And, it gets even cooler. Not only does God understand my needs and desires, He meets those needs
with good things. Psalm 103:5 says that the Lord "sat-
isfies your desires with good things so that your youth
is renewed like the eagles." In the case of my Twister

episode with Jacob, my youth was subdued, rather than renewed, I suppose. But the point remains the same: We serve an omnipotent, creative, and mighty God who desires to meet the needs of His people with what is best and right for us. We don't need to work more to impress Him; we simply need to be still and ask.

Look closely at Psalm 46:10. "**Enough**! Now know that I am God." As we obey the first command—Enough! Cease Striving! Be Still! Stop!—we are freed to see the second part play out. As we stop attempting to do on our own, we acknowledge the One who has not only the authority to make that command, but also the ability to back up that authority with almighty power. If we truly know that He is God, and believe all that means, that first command is unnecessary. If we behold our Father and understand our abilities in comparison to His and believe the promises He's made to us, we will be still. We will cease striving because we will be in awe. In knowing God, we know there is nothing we can do to add to what He has already done. We can stand, still, and confidently proclaim: *My All in All, here in the love of Christ I stand.*

Hear God whisper, as He continues to whisper to me: **Cease striving. Let me show you a better way. My Way. On your own, you are not enough, but I AM. I am the bread of life and I have made you who you are. I have more in store for you than you could ever ask for or imagine. Abundant Life. Look to Me to rain it down on you.**

"Is the Lord's arm too short?"

BACK TO THE ISRAELITES. I don't mean to pick on them. Lord knows they had been through a lot. But, they were kind of whiny. It's probably why I relate so well to them. They whined about hunger and God provided manna. Further along on their journey, the manna became a problem. The consistency of God's daily provision became too mundane.

Let me show you. I encourage you to read the whole account in Numbers 11:4-35, but I will offer snippets below.

> The rabble with them began to crave other food, and again the Israelites started wailing and said, "If only we had meat to eat! We remember the fish we ate in Egypt at no cost— also the cucumbers, melons, leeks, onions,

and garlic. But now we have lost our appetite; we never see anything but this manna!"

[The Lord said,] "Tell the people: 'Consecrate yourselves in preparation for tomorrow when you will eat meat. The Lord heard you when you wailed, "If only we had meat to eat! We were better off in Egypt!" Now the Lord will give you meat, and you will eat it. You will not eat it for just one day, or two days, or five, ten or twenty days, but for a whole month—until it comes out of your nostrils and you loathe it—because you have rejected the Lord, who is among you, and have wailed before Him saying, "Why did we ever leave Egypt?"'

But Moses said, "Here I am among six hundred thousand men on foot, and you say, 'I will give them meat to eat for a whole month!' Would they have enough if flocks and herds were slaughtered for them? Would they have enough if all the fish in the sea were caught for them?"

The Lord answered Moses, "Is the Lord's arm too short? You will now see whether or not what I say will come true for you."

Now a wind went out from the Lord and drove quail in from the sea. It brought them down all around the camp to about three feet above the ground, as far as a day's walk in any direction. All that day and night and all the next day the people went out and gathered quail. No one gathered less than ten homers. Then they spread them out all around the camp. But

while the meat was still between their teeth
and before it could be consumed, the anger of
the Lord burned against the people...[1]

Not to miss the greater purpose of the story, but
don't you hate it when you get food stuck between your
teeth? I bet the manna never got stuck. Just saying.

I don't often think I sound like God when I parent,
but this instruction of His sounds a little bit like something I would say. *What's that, children? You don't like the
food I'm offering? Oh, you want meat? I CAN HEAR YOU
BACK THERE! You better consecrate yourself, Son. 'Cause
Immabout to give you what you want. And you will eat it.
FOREVER!*

"Consecrate yourselves" can mean "sanctify
yourselves," but it can also mean "Prepare to meet
thy Father."[2] It's possible I've said those exact words
to my kids.

Moses responds very humanly, doesn't he? *God,
let's not get carried away. I get it—you're angry. But I'm
down here with a lot of people. We don't have that kind of
meat laying around. Do the math. You're going to need to
dial it back a notch.*

Even after all they had been through, the Hebrews
and their leadership still had more to learn about the
Manna Provider.

The group must have been excited when the new
food came in. Certainly, when the wind flew in the
quail until it was waist-high in every direction for a

---

1 Numbers 11:4–6, 18–23, 31–34
2 Rev. Joseph Benson, *Commentary of the Old and New Testaments* (New
York: Carlton & Porter, 1857), http://biblehub.com/commentaries/benson/
numbers/11.htm.

day's walk, they knew they had enough. In fact, Psalm 78: 27–29 describes the experience this way:

> He rained meat down on them like dust, flying birds like sand on the seashore. He made them come down inside their camp, all around their tents. They ate till they had *more than enough*, for he had given them what they craved (emphasis mine).

They must have been ecstatic: *We got what we wanted!* But quickly, they realized that all the meat would not collect and prepare itself, and they set about the work of gathering their food. Rather than gathering the "matter of the day in its day" as they did with manna, the people gathered the meat "all day and night and all the next day" in order to deal with all the excess. In fact, their hard work paid off. They were able to gather one hundred times what they needed—*How self-sufficient are we*, they must have thought.[3]

God had (again) provided enough for each person. More than that, actually. God demonstrated to Moses and to all the Hebrews that His arm is not too short to provide more than enough for the six hundred thousand men in addition to the women and children. More than Moses ever imagined that He could.

The first time the Israelites complained about food, way back at the beginning of the journey, God was not angry. They had a need and He provided for that. In

3 A homer is a "heap, the largest of dry measures, ... [and] equals 10 ephahs." And we all now know that an omer—the amount they needed—is only one tenth of a ephah. See www.biblestudytools.com/dictionary/homer.

fact, He caused their hunger so that they would need His provision.[4] This second time, however, He had been providing for that need, but their hearts were demanding the way in which they wanted to be provided for. They wanted what they craved and were choosing to be unsatisfied with God's provision. They had their collective will, and they wanted to have their way. There was a lesson in obedience and trust: God's arm is not too short to accomplish anything. But, **where there is His Will, there is His Way.**

I am not suggesting that we are disobedient when we lay our hearts' desires before God. He loves nothing more than when we seek Him. I'm suggesting that as we do that, we must be willing to present them with an open hand. What we think or feel we want, no matter how earnestly, may not lead to the abundant life that God has for us. Like the Hebrews having to work day and night simply to gather that which they thought they wanted, that which we crave may be messing negatively with our lives in ways we don't even realize.

Now ABOUT THESE RABBLE ROUSERS. Rabble rousers—people who attempt to incite a group to anger in order to effect change—have their place. Sometimes, the status quo needs to change. But what I find interesting in this case is who the "rabble" are. The particular group in this passage are outsiders, a group of non-Israelites who had followed the Israelites out of Egypt. My study bible notes, "Those who did not know the Lord and His mercies incited those who did know

---

4 See Deuteronomy 8:3

Him to rebel against Him."[5] The rabble, not the Israelites, first craved other food. Those content in God's provision were led toward discontentment by turning their eyes and ears toward "others." Satan is not new to this game. He so cunningly drums up drama as a way to entice our eyes away from God's enough for us.

This is a classic case of the grass is always greener on the other side of the desert. With a little help, the Israelites again remembered their time in captivity as a period of life where they dined on meat and fresh veggies *at no cost* to them. That slavery thing? A minor inconvenience in light of the wonderful spread they received every night. The manna was also provided to them without cost, so I'm confused that the free nature of the food became the focus of their lamenting. Did they think God was being cheap? That He was holding out on them? I don't know what their thoughts were, but God knew He was being rejected.

Of course, the rabble had not been slaves. Their journey, while the same geographically, started from a very different place in their hearts. The rabble had not experienced God's merciful deliverance; they were just along for the ride. The Israelites may not have understood the greater purpose of their journey, but they were connected to it. The rabble were not. Without a connection to a God-ordained purpose, the journey was about eating manna and wandering around for them. I bet that got old. In the same way, without greater purpose, this journey called life would be about getting the most and best we can for ourselves, too.

---

5 *The NIV Study Bible*, 10th Anniversary Edition (Grand Rapids: Zondervan Publishing House, 1995).

In C.S. Lewis' satirical writing, *The Screwtape Letters*, we gain fictional insight into how Satan loves to use others to subtly cause discontentment. Screwtape, one of Satan's chief demons, instructs his nephew, Wormwood, who is new to the evil business:

> The man who truly and disinterestedly enjoys any one thing in the world, for its own sake, and without caring two-pence what other people say about it, is by that very fact forearmed against some of our subtlest modes of attack."[6]

Satan will use the things of this world, including the people of this world, to try to pull us away from our Provider in a hundred subtle ways every day. If you've broken out of bondage from something, you better believe he's going to bring back a strong selective memory from time to time, and often during a vulnerable time, of something about that bondage-creating thing that provided comfort, excitement, prestige—something for which you long.

For the Hebrews, they had the memories of those comfort foods. I cannot even imagine how good and comforting a steamy pot of stew or hot plate of fish and veggies must have tasted to them after a long day of back-breaking labor in the brickyards. It likely provided a small opportunity for rest. A moment to cease their labors and feel filled.

It wasn't that the food they were craving was bad;

---

6 C.S. Lewis, *The Screwtape Letters* (New York: Harpers Collins, 1942, Copyright restored 1996), 66.

heck, fish and veggies is a dietician's dream diet. The problem was that their eyes had been turned, and had thus turned their hearts, into an attitude of ingratitude. The desire for something else made them "lose their appetite" for the gifts of manna from God. He wanted to be that which offered fulfillment. God knew that the Hebrews were rejecting His provision—and therefore Him—for a temporal comfort that could not provide lasting contentment. He needed to reset their appetites so they would crave that which came from Him.

In the same way, God knows that we sometimes have things in our lives—certain "comfort foods" upon which we have relied—that are keeping us from depending on Him and growing closer to Him. We are looking to other things to bring contentment in a way that only He can. If we are, they are not going to provide abundant life. They are weighing us down, holding us back, taking up too much of our time.

These "comfort foods" may not be bad things; we may not even recognize their effect on our lives. But God does. He knows when our appetites need to be reset, when the trappings of this world are causing us to reject Him. Yes, Satan is cunning. Yes, Satan is wily and persistent. He reminds us, day after day, of things and emotions and strongholds that appear to be insurmountable. We become weary. Perhaps the craving seems to be getting bigger. We long for that which comforts, for that which makes us feel full. Maybe we feel like God's not so big or has started to forget our struggles and doesn't have our best interests in mind after all. *He's not strong enough. Or He's holding out on us. It has to be one or the other.* Slowly, subtly, Satan encourages us to lend our ear to the rabble. *It shouldn't be this hard*, suggests the World.

Dear Friend, hear this: God's arm is not too short to enter into any area of your life which threatens to enslave you. He has not forgotten you or stopped listening. In the last chapter we talked about how God loves you just the way you are. You do not need to be any more than you already are to be loved perfectly by God. But because He loves you as much as He does, He is not going to let you stay where you are. He is here to journey with you toward something more. The journey may not be easy and it may not take the direction you expect, but His Way leads to abundant life. Trust in His strength and rest in His loving kindness toward those for whom He provides.

Don't Get Hung Up on That

THIS THING I'M GOING TO WRITE should go without saying because we all "know" it, but truth bears repeating: God knows you are not perfect. If you have ever said or heard someone else say, "God knows I'm not perfect," it's true. He does. He's okay with that. He expects that. In fact, He sent His Son to take care of that for you. And to take care of that for me. And for that jerk who seems unlovable. We are sinful, every last one of us. There is refining work to be done.

This human imperfection started a long time ago, and it's caused shame nearly from the beginning. Adam and Eve lived nakedly before the Lord, until they sinned. After eating from the tree of the knowledge of good and evil, they became aware of their naked state. That nakedness in front of God scared them and they hid from Him as He walked through the garden.[1]

These two humans had the chance to go on a garden stroll with God, to talk directly with Him about anything on their hearts, but their human imperfection caused shame and created a separation. It broke the relationship. But notice, Adam and Eve hid, and God sought them out. God continued to pursue them. He already knew what they had done; He loved them still.

Adam and Eve were quickly in over their heads.

---

1 I encourage you to read the full account in Genesis 3.

To an unknowing human mind, one seemingly simple bad choice had horrible, eternal consequences. It could easily be called The Worst Choice of All Time. They didn't know how to fix it, because they couldn't. So the bad decisions continued. (My kids are so related to these people.) Instead of turning toward God, they turned away.

Since everything comes back to pee and poop at our house these days, let me tell you a little potty training misstep we had. I mean, a literal misstep. One of our blessed boys had gone Number 2 in his underwear. My personal potty-training favorite. Geoff was on doody duty and went to clean him up. Geoff didn't realize that one Number 2 had fallen onto the floor when he was cleaning the boy up. Geoff also did not realize that he had stepped on the runaway with his tennis shoe. What made the mess so unfortunate is that Geoff didn't realize he had stepped on it until he had crossed our carpeted living room and was halfway up the stairs. Not even our nature fresh air freshener could cover up that "nature-fresh" smell. A small, contained bathroom mess soon affected our entire house.

OUR MESSES OFTEN MULTIPLY, don't they? We start heading down the wrong path, and before we know it, the place where we end up is so far from where we intended to go. The nature of sin is such that if we don't seek forgiveness and repent, it stays with us and often starts to stink up other parts of our life. (Satan loves this exponential return on his salami-slicing thievery.)

Perhaps you are familiar with the story of King David and Bathsheba. It's a scandalous biblical story. It is also the basis for the Veggie Tales movie *King George and the Ducky*.[2] The movie has a much less scandalous storyline, one that entails a bath-loving king and his coveting of all the rubber ducks, but the message of redemption is the same. In David's life, what began as his lustful thoughts toward a married woman led to adultery, which led to more lies, a cowardly plot to murder, and a significant betrayal. Had David repented of his unclean thoughts, the path of destruction may have ended. But instead, as I often do in my life, David made excuses to justify his sin, which kept him on the path that ended up not only in the death of Bathsheba's first husband, but also cost the life of David and Bathsheba's first son.

Now, however, to what could be the ending to any story ever told that began with someone's sin—God's forgiveness! There is no sin that God cannot wash away. When David was confronted with his sin, he pleaded with God to forgive him: "Wash away all my iniquity and cleanse me from my sin."[3] And in knowing God, David had confidence in his request: "Cleanse me with hyssop, and I will be clean; wash me, and I will be whiter than snow."[4]

As humans, we will sin. Even as we do this, in our worst moments, God loves us. He is right beside us, waiting for us to turn to Him. Continue to hand those areas in your life in which you struggle and that you are striving to control on your own over to God. Pray boldly for His work in your life. Notice that David did not

2 Veggie Tales: *King George and the Ducky*. Dir. Mike Nawrocki. Big Idea, 2000. DVD.
3 Psalm 51:2
4 Psalm 51:7

ask for a gentle washing. Hyssop was used for purifica-
tion, such as in the cleansing of a leper. David did not
ask simply to be made clean; like a leper, he wanted
to be cleansed to the core so that the crippling effects
of the sin were completely and permanently removed.
Please do not read this as fire and brimstone preaching; please, please, please hear the great hope of which
I speak. God wants His hands on the dirtiest, most vulnerable, most despairing, hopeless parts of your life.
And He doesn't just want to make them clean enough.
He wants to walk in, command "Enough!" and hyssop
the beegeebees out of the place. Until nothing but His
authority reigns. We will never be perfect, but God's
purging has eternal purpose.

**There is a difference between allowing God to
purge the things in your life that need to be refined,
and getting hung up on the things that He intends to
use for His glory.** It can be tempting to use our failings
and perceived weaknesses as an excuse to stay where
we are. But our journey goes beyond here, right where
we are.

You may be in a place where your journey doesn't
make sense. Your life may feel purposeless, and the
wandering has gotten old. It may feel like you are getting nowhere or that others have figured life out and
you are left spinning your wheels. Or, perhaps you
feel like you've journeyed to right where you thought
you wanted to be, but now that you've arrived, it still
doesn't feel like Enough. If that's you, never forget
who is leading you. Keep your eyes focused on Him. He
is trustworthy. Ask Him to provide direction for your
next step, and then take it.

Or, perhaps you have not been following God, and now you feel too far from Him to get back. Hear this: regardless of where you have been, where you are, or where you think you are headed, you are never more than one footstep away from following Him. Never. If that's you, turn your eyes to focus on Him. Let Him lead you on a journey with purpose.

The Manna Provider has not changed. God can still provide everything we need. God can overcome all that overwhelms us. His arm is not too short. I want you to sit with this for a minute. Think about those things in your life that you get hung up on. Big things and little things. Think of those obstacles that threaten your ability to seek His purposes. Hear those thoughts that taunt you to feel like you are not enough. Feel that paralyzing feeling that stops you. Acknowledge that need to strive to feel like Enough for God. Now hear this word about all of those things: **Jesus did not hang on the cross for you to get hung up on that.** Whatever "that" is for you, its power is less than the power of the cross. Guaranteed. Jesus' arms—outstretched wide on the cross—are not too short. The Bread of Life who promises life to the full is stronger than our greatest stronghold.

God has a calling for your life, a purpose for every day. Satan knows that. Satan has chosen to make it his life's work to try to thwart God's purposes. Satan loves to draw our attention to our weaknesses and create discontentment in order to use it against us. To paralyze us from doing our thing. Satan would love for you to focus on your "that." It may be a sin that you think is unforgivable. It may be a lack of confidence. It may be a perceived (or actual) lack of skill. God, on the other hand, is not particularly interested in these things. Because He knows He is more than "that." And He will be Enough to overcome "that." Not just one time, but time and time again. Take heart and keep reading: your "that" is authenticity, and it might just be the most important thing you have to offer. Embrace your human authenticity. Be who you are, right where you are. God is doing a mighty work in you. And He is pleased with you. There may be some purging on your journey, some weaknesses that are revealed, some discontentment that you want restored, but know that you are God's workmanship and there is beauty in every step of the process. **That beautiful imperfect brokenness makes you, you, and you, as you are, is exactly who God has come to rescue.**

identity

"I will take you as my own people"

We are nearing the end. I will miss the Hebrews. They have shown me that humans are unique, but the human experience has many commonalities. Spending time studying their gathering of enough has shown me that the spiritual journey of God's people, known simply as life, is very important to Him. He shows up faithfully for it.

Over their time in slavery, the Hebrews had lost their true identity, wrecking their confidence not only in themselves, but more importantly in their God. They no longer felt like God's chosen people; they felt ignored. They had become a people of captivity, people more comfortable with wailing than worshiping. **The Israelites needed to be reminded of who they were, as defined by whose they were.**

I'm stepping back in Scripture a bit to the place

where the Israelites were really first tested by Moses'
and Aaron's arrival. We are stepping back to the period
after Moses and Aaron had told Pharaoh to let God's
people go, and Pharaoh had responded by increasing
their daily quota of bricks. The Israelites' "matter of
a day in its day" had become harder to bear, and they
wanted Moses to leave. *Thanks for nothing, Moses. We
will take it from here.*

Moses questioned God on what He was doing, and
in fact pointed out to God that He was not doing much.
In Exodus 5:23, he said: "Ever since I went to Pharaoh
to speak in Your name, he has brought trouble upon
this people, and You have not rescued Your people at
all." Moses, the self-proclaimed humblest man on
Earth, took the opportunity to point out to Almighty
God that all of this was being done *in His name* and by
the way, *not sure You've noticed, but the Hebrews are still
not free.* Humble and subtle, indeed.

God offered Moses a pep talk to bring back to the
Israelites:

> Therefore, say to the Israelites: "I am the
> Lord, and I will bring you out from under the
> yoke of the Egyptians. I will free you from be-
> ing slaves to them, and I will redeem you with
> an outstretched arm and with mighty acts of
> judgment. I will take you as My own people,
> and I will be your God. Then you will know
> that I am the Lord your God, who brought
> you out from under the yoke of the Egyptians.
> And I will bring you to the land I swore with
> uplifted hand to give to Abraham, to Isaac

and to Jacob. I will give it to you as a posses-
sion. I am the Lord.

Moses reported this to the Israelites, but
they did not listen to him because of their dis-
couragement and cruel bondage.[1]

The Israelites had lost that identity, in their own
eyes, as God's chosen people. Rather, they were slaves
under the yoke of the Egyptians. They were disheart-
ened and not interested in journeys that, so far, had
only made their lives harder. Perhaps it was easier
simply to stay who they were, where they were. Slavery had led them to a place in which they had become
literally dis-couraged; their courage had been taken
from them.

God knew the heart condition of the Israelites.
The authority who had been dictating their Enough
for each day—Pharaoh—had not been trustworthy.
Everything had been about what the Israelites would
do for Pharaoh, because of who he was. In this message to His people, God declared to the Israelites what
He would do for them, because of who He was. God
proclaimed the actions by which He would show His
people that their God was trustworthy and dependable. "Trustworthy" and "dependable" seem inadequate to describe the Creator of All Things, but as in
any relationship, those qualities are everything. The
bondage of the Israelites was so much more than a
physical bondage. They may not have even realized
how much they identified as slaves. But a powerful,
yet loving authority upon whom they could trust was

1 Exodus 6:6-9

115

a foreign concept to His people as they had not seen such authority for generations. God was what they needed Him to be first—trustworthy—so that they might learn how to trust.

To show the Hebrews who they were in Him, God met them where they were. **God was at work; they simply needed to show up for the journey, trusting in that work.** Their Egyptian exodus would have been a much different story if it had gone smoothly. As easily as God hardened Pharaoh's heart, He might have softened it, like He did the other Egyptians. He might have allowed Moses to simply show up, make His request, and march out with God's chosen people. But that wouldn't have made for a very good story. He used Pharaoh's hardened heart and the subsequent plagues to start to create a new common narrative of God's chosen people. *God did all of these things for us.* The Israelites could begin to see themselves, and thereby identify themselves, as a people whose God was willing to fight for them.

Even in the identifying title of God's chosen people, God is the subject doing the action and His people are the object being acted upon. He chose them. They were not chosen due to any worth based on their own merit. They were who they were because of who they were to Him. God was intimately involved in their identity. It is why they needed to "follow His instructions" and "know that He is the Lord your God." They needed to re-learn who they most authentically were. And so, God "took" the Hebrews as His own people and showed them who they were.

Not to grammar-geek-out on you, but some good

old-fashioned sentence diagramming of His pep talk reveals God's game plan of who would do what and why in this process. God is the subject of every single sentence but one. Four times in this passage God refers to who He is. Three of these times, He states simply who He is: "I am the Lord." The fourth time, He defines who He is to the Hebrews: "I will be your God." He makes it personal.

God's plan certainly involves the Hebrews as well; He speaks about them as "you" eight times. Seven of those times "you" is the direct object of the sentence which is being acted upon by God: bring you out, free you, redeem you, take you, give to you. His game plan offers promises to the Hebrews which, when fulfilled, will show that He is faithful. Only one time "You," again referring to the Hebrews, is the subject. The action they will take is in response to what God will have already done: "I will be your God. *Then*, you will know that I am the Lord your God." God acts first, and then they respond. God is who He is first, and then the Hebrews become who they will be in response.

And so, in the very beginning of this relationship to be built upon trust, they set out. No longer Egyptian slaves, but certainly not yet free, the Hebrews began to journey. And as they journeyed, they started to see that they were indeed a people for whom their God provided. The provision of manna slowly, day by day, taught them to identify as such: *We are a people who go out and gather the enough each day that God has provided.* More specifically, *I am a person for whom my God provides.*

This identity is the same one He offers to us: *I am a person for whom my God provides.*

WE BECOME THE TRUEST VERSIONS **of ourselves when we recognize that our identity begins with who we are in Him.** We take our cue from our Creator. The more we seek and depend on Him to order our day, the clearer sense we gain of who He created us to be. As He shows us our matter of the day in its day—our Enough—He shows us who we uniquely are. We learn about our authentic selves, and there is great contentment in being just as we are intended to be before our God.

C.S. Lewis' book, *The Screwtape Letters,* offers a great perspective on the freedom to be ourselves as we draw near to the One who created us to be who we are in the first place. Satan's demon says this about God (referred to in this quote as "the Enemy") and His desire for our identity to be rooted in Him so we can be most authentically ourselves:

> Of course I know that the Enemy also wants to detach men from themselves, but in a different way. Remember always, that He really likes the little vermin, and sets an absurd value on the distinctness of every one of them. When He talks of their losing their selves, He only means abandoning the clamour of self-will; once they have done that, He really gives them back all their personality, and boasts (I am afraid, sincerely), that when they are wholly His they will be more themselves than ever. Hence, while [God] is delighted to see them sacrificing even their innocent will to His, He hates to see them

drifting away from their own nature for any other reason.[2]

God has designed us to journey as a tribe, not a herd. As we seek Him, He never intends to make us less of ourselves. Our increased dependence on Him is not designed to lessen that which makes us uniquely us. In fact, as we draw closer to our Creator, we gain a better sense of who we are. And possibly, who we are not. We begin to see ourselves through the eyes and purposes God has for us.

AARON, MY OLDER BROTHER, was only a year ahead of me in school. In high school, he was bullied by a group of guys because he had taken the starting position in basketball away from one of their friends. I remember one game vividly: Aaron was the best three-point shooter on our team. On this particular occasion, however, he shot and missed. One of the bullies was standing right in front of me in the stands, and he heckled Aaron. I was livid! A friend of mine who was standing next to me heard the comment, and, without hesitation, whacked him on the back of the head. He turned around, saw me standing there, and turned back around without saying a word. I took all of the credit for the head-whack, and I'm not going to lie, it felt great!

A few weeks later, after another basketball game, Aaron and I were driving home with some friends. Lo and behold, on the side of the road stood this same bully. Aaron saw him and, without hesitation, pulled over

---

2 C.S. Lewis, *The Screwtape Letters* (New York: Harpers Collins, 1942, Copyright restored 1996), 65.

and picked him up. Apparently, his friends had decided to ditch him and he was left with no way home. All the way home, I was thinking, *Aaron, here's your chance. Work harder! Act more like this guy thinks "cool" people act.* But, Aaron kept acting just like normal. When Aaron dropped him off, the guy mumbled a sheepish "Thank you," and hurried out the door.

Aaron was more concerned with getting that guy home than he was with getting even. Now, to be honest, I will always feel great satisfaction when I think about that head-whack because I think he deserved it. But Aaron giving him a ride home was so much cooler simply because the bully didn't deserve it, at least not from Aaron.

I've talked to Aaron about this incident. He hardly remembers the event in his life, but it was a defining moment in mine. I was baffled by the whole situation, Aaron's actions included. I could not understand why anyone would pick on the person I'd admired more than anyone else in the world. But as I reflect back, I realize that Aaron's confidence is what I admired, and it's also likely what led those boys to pick on him. Aaron showed me that people with a solid sense of their authentic identity in Christ can be self-confident precisely because their confidence lies not in their self, but rather in the God who made them who they are. He didn't need to listen to the words others said about him, try to change their opinion, or get revenge to "even the score," because he wasn't listening to them for his identity. He was just being authentically Aaron.

Identity is a powerful construct. That which defines us—that by which we identify ourselves—affects how we act, how we make decisions, and even how we think about ourselves. Satan encourages us to base our identity on that which paralyzes us from acting. When the Hebrews identified themselves based on the cruel bondage they had endured under the yoke of the Egyptians, they lacked the courage to trust God to deliver them. When Moses was called to lead the Hebrews, he struggled to move past his inability to speak clearly. If our perceived greatest weaknesses become that which most defines who we are, we will lose our courage to step out in what God would have us do.

IF, ON THE OTHER HAND, we establish our identity in who we are in God, we allow Him to define the role those weaknesses and insecurities have in our lives. When we define who we are by whose we are, we create an identity based on He who will never change. *I am not God, but I can depend on God. I am one of His chosen people for whom He provides. I am one of those people for whom Jesus died on the cross so that I might know abundant life. I am one who finds Enough in Him.*

We will talk about the place God has for those weaknesses and insecurities in a little bit.

Authenticity: Be Who You Are

IN WRITING THIS BOOK, I drank a lot of coffee. Actually, that's not true. I drank a lot of lattes with a little bit of coffee product in them, but mostly milk and some form of sugar. At one point, I told the barista I wanted something creamy, but perhaps a little healthier for me. She suggested I switch out the milk I have in my latte for half and half. I looked at her quizzically. She admitted that it wasn't exactly healthier, but it would be creamy. In the spirit of half and half, I rationalized that it fit half my criteria and ordered one. I actually ordered it with half the half and half. It may sound like a complicated math question, but the answer is simple: a drink made with half and half is called a breve, and it's delicious.

As I write this, I'm choking down a cup of actual coffee made drinkable only by adding the last bit of whole milk in our house (which is supposed to be for my daughter—it's okay, she's resilient). *Why bother*, you ask? Because I want to be a coffee drinker. I want people to know me as a coffee purist who doesn't even leave room for cream. But I'm not. If I'm honest, I would keep the cream and lose the coffee.

Part of my desired desire to love coffee is that I love coffee shops. I love the vibe, and the deep thought and quality conversation that you can practically smell mingling with the coffee grounds as you step in the door. I want to be among these people. So, I go to coffee shops, but I feel like such a poser. It's just not hipster to order a drink with equal parts coffee and sugar.

On a family vacation to Estes Park, Colorado, I left early one morning to try out a hip-looking coffee shop I had seen. I was nervous because its website had a "purist" vibe, and you know how people are who live near the mountains. I didn't know how they'd receive a sugar lover like myself.

My drink of choice at that time was Starbucks' Caramel Macchiato. Although caramel is in its title, I hoped "macchiato" was a legitimate coffee drink, with my addition of caramel simply adding a touch of sweet refinement.[1] I hesitantly approached the counter, but when I looked up at the menu, I noticed they had a macchiato on the menu—*how legit am I?* I was a purist after all, or this particular coffee shop had sold out to the masses; I suppose either way I got the drink I wanted. I confidently approached the barista, and loudly declared, "I will have a caramel macchiato with a single shot please." The barista smiled, and then asked (a little too loudly for my liking), "Now, do you want the traditional macchiato, or the one that Starbucks makes? You know, the latte that's just basically a really sweet drink."

Speaking much more quietly now, I asked her to explain the difference, hoping the difference was subtle. It wasn't. *Well, shoot.* I had a choice to make: Was I going to be the poser purist and drink the

---

1 No helpful information here, reader. Just wanted to check your diligence in reading.

espresso with a touch of foam (gag), or own up to my sweet-loving tendencies and order the Starbucks vanilla-syruped latte with an extra drizzle of caramel syrup? I mumbled that I wanted the second one and then to make matters worse, she asked for my name. This customer service technique, ironically one often associated with Starbucks, is designed to make an individual feel unique and important, but in this particular instance, it felt more like a shaming strategy. So I stood in the corner and awaited the barista's announcement that my drink was ready to claim: "Elise, super sugary poser macchiato."

I don't pretend to understand the theology of how God created me and how sin has affected that as it relates to my desire for a hot sugary beverage. Perhaps it doesn't. But God continues to use these silly examples in my life to show me His truth for my life: *Just be who you are. Enough of trying to be like someone else or to follow another's journey. Be the You I have created. I have created you uniquely, for a unique purpose, with unique struggles, unique gifts, unique taste buds. Let me show you what and why and when.*

So many of us go through life wanting to be unique, to stand out, to be noteworthy; all the while wanting to look like another, trying to act like others, working to have the same things as those around us. And God is shaking His Holy Head, thinking, *I have made you unique. Go, be unique. Own that quirk and milk it for all it's worth. Nevertheless. You seek to be something else.*

He created us and He is not finished with us yet. And yes, those things we don't like about ourselves— those ways we respond, those quirks that annoy, those hard-wired behaviors, those thighs—they may never go away. I may very well fumble my words when I speak until I speak my last words, but that doesn't mean He doesn't have a purpose in my fumbling. **Our greatest offering is the discombobulated version of who we are in each and every moment. There is no more authentic gift that we can offer.**

God intends to walk with us through triumphs, challenges, struggles, lessons, victories, and the mundane—all things that will shape us in different ways. It's a paradox that in every situation we are to be who we are so that we can be changed by that experience into who God would have us become. **By living authentically, we acknowledge that our Creator knows what He is doing. I glorify Him by being me. And there is great purpose and significance simply in bringing glory to God in whatever He calls us to do.**

purpose

"Please send someone
else to do it."

THERE'S ONE INSTRUMENTAL CHARACTER that we haven't talked about much to this point: Moses. He's so fascinating to me because he played such an instrumental leadership role in the history of God's chosen people. But he went about it so hesitantly, so reluctantly. So much like a normal human might. One might suggest that he struggled with discontentment in his life. His life offers a great example of an individual stuck in a circumstance that doesn't make sense until the moment it makes absolute sense. Moses was the Hebrew-born man raised in Pharaoh's palace, who fled from Pharaoh only to come back and lead the Hebrew people away from Pharaoh as well. He was the man with a speech impediment who would speak on behalf of all the Hebrews. He was the humble man who mediated between God and His people.

When God approached Moses by way of a burning bush, Moses thought He had the wrong guy. He asked "Who am I, that I should go to Pharaoh and bring the Israelites out of Egypt?"[1] God continued to reassure Moses that He would be with him, and that God already knew how the whole thing would go down. Moses responded, "What if they do not believe me or listen to me and say, 'The Lord did not appear to you?'"[2] God patiently reassured. Then Moses got more specific, "O Lord, I have never been eloquent, neither in the past nor since you have spoken to your servant. I am slow of speech and tongue."[3] I love this one. *Lord, we've been talking about this for a full five minutes, and I'm still not a great speaker.* The Lord redirects: "Who gave man his mouth? Who makes him deaf or mute? Who gives him sight or makes him blind? Is it not I, the Lord? Now go; I will help you speak and will teach you what to say."[4]

But Moses said, "O Lord, please send someone else to do it."[5]

God was not surprised by Moses' reaction. He had already prompted Aaron to come and meet Moses so that Aaron could speak to Pharaoh. But God was not going to let Moses focus on his weakness when God had a specific purpose for his life.

Throughout his interactions with the Israelites, as well as with Pharaoh, Moses continued to focus and fret about his inability to speak effectively.

---

1 Exodus 3:11
2 Exodus 4:1
3 Exodus 4:10
4 Exodus 4:11
5 Exodus 4:13

Then the Lord said to Moses, "Go, tell Pharaoh king of Egypt to let the Israelites go out of his country." But Moses said to the Lord, "If the Israelites will not listen to me, why would Pharaoh listen to me, since I speak with faltering lips?"[6]...

[God] said to [Moses], "I am the Lord. Tell Pharaoh king of Egypt everything I tell you."

But Moses said to the Lord, "Since I speak with faltering lips, why would Pharaoh listen to me?"

Then the Lord said to Moses, "See, I have made you like God to Pharaoh, and your brother Aaron will be your prophet. You are to say everything I command you, and your brother Aaron is to tell Pharaoh to let the Israelites go out of his country."[7]

For someone who thought he was a fumbling communicator, Moses communicated crystal clearly about his inability to speak well. Despite the direct conversation with God, Moses hesitated. He even tried to explain to God that which God was obviously overlooking. *You don't understand how inadequate I am God.* When God was not dissuaded by that, he simply asked for God to pick someone else. *I am not enough to do what You are asking of me, Lord.* **But God had a perfect plan for Moses' imperfect skills. God focused on God's power, while Moses focused on Moses' weakness. Moses was not enough. But God was.**

6 Exodus 6:10-12
7 Exodus 6:29—7:2

How ironic is it that we are called to draw close to God, when in so doing, standing in awe of His perfection and power illuminates our weaknesses and imperfections all the more clearly? It makes me wonder: How do we find contentment in a God who knows these imperfections of ours, even as drawing closer shows us more of His awesome perfection?

We do, because that is how God designed it. He has redeemed us and uses our imperfections to bring glory to His perfection. We can be content in His purpose for our lives, even as we are not enough to accomplish them on our own, because we are not called to accomplish them on our own. We are called to be ourselves and to let God work through us. We have been made uniquely to bring Him glory uniquely. And even though we will never be enough, that imperfection is perfect in Him. **We can let the cracks of our human authenticity be the window through which God's glory shines most clearly through us. We can be content day by day knowing that we are never enough, and that's God's perfect design. Because He always is.** I'm so excited about this; let me show you what I mean.

WE HAVE COME to the last definition of "Enough," which has been the most powerful for me. Remember how I told you that I read John 14:8 the day God whispered "Enough" to drown out the negative voices hammering away in my head, but also to speak life into the book that He called me to write? This was not a coincidence, Friends. Think about this. I had been plodding through the Bible from the beginning for four years. Four years. I was in the book of John. Pretty sure

I finished the Old Testament at the end of the last year. It was November, friends. It was November, and I had gotten to the last of the four gospels. Which is also the number of precious children I have, so there you have it. All this to say, my Bible reading process has been methodical in the approach—picking up where I left off in reading cover to cover – but haphazard in the application—starting and stopping countless times in the last four years. And yet on that particular day, the frustration I felt brought me to call upon God for His help and He directed me to pick up once again where I had left off. God had orchestrated each passage I'd read in the last four years to allow me to read John 14:8 at that moment: "Lord, show us the Father and that will be **enough** for us." I love the amazing connections and rich word study that happen by studying His Word, but I love this verse for its powerful simplicity. Witty and profound have their place, but God does not require window dressing. He is enough for us.

I hope y'all are word nerds like me, because if you are, you will enjoy this next connection as much as I do; it's so fitting with what else He has shown us about Enough.

The word "enough" in John 14:8 is the Greek word, "ἀρκεῖ."[8] This word occurs in this form only one other time in the New Testament, which is in 2 Corinthians 12:9. In this passage, Paul had asked for a particular weakness he struggled with to be removed from him, but the Lord refused. Instead the Lord responded, "My grace is **enough** for you, for my power is made perfect

---

8 George Wigram, *Englishman's Greek Concordance of the New Testament*, www.biblehub.com/greek/arkei_714.htm.

133

in weakness." "Enough" in this context means "suffi-cient." John 14:8 could read, "Show us the Father and that will be sufficient for us." Similarly, some transla-tions actually translate 2 Corinthians 12:9 as "My grace is sufficient for you."⁹

So, I've got to be honest: When I see the word "sufficient," it doesn't exactly pull at my heartstrings. It's not a word one would use to describe a trip of a lifetime, for instance; it's more like a word one would use to describe the efficiency of their dishwasher. I'd rather have God describe His grace as "overpower-ing" or "awe-inspiring" - something that looks great blasted on the screen during worship. After all, grace is His greatest gift to us. "Sufficient," on the other hand, feels to me like "barely enough."

If I'm going to be called to carry out hard, out-side-my-box, not-my-expectation, fear-causing-eter-nal-purposes with my day, "sufficient" does not feel like it's going to cut it. That's not going to be enough to overcome whatever is holding me back. I hear Satan once again taunting: *Is God's enough, enough? Barely. You. Want. More. You. Need. More.* These salami-slicing jabs nudge me toward striving just a wee bit more—either to try to solve it on my own, or try to overcome my weaknesses by myself (hear my toddler rally cry: "I DO IT SELF!"). Or maybe just to stay discouraged and not even try.

But God has written the formula, and it cannot be derived into any other form: **His sufficient grace plus my weakness equals His power perfected. My weak-**

---

9 See the New International Version, English Standard Version, New American Standard Bible, King James Bible.

nesses, my struggles, my not-enoughs are a key component to my purpose in glorifying God. They make me who I am. The rest of 2 Corinthians 12:9, along with verse 10, continues:

> "My grace is enough for you, for my power is made perfect in weakness." So then, I will boast most gladly about my weaknesses, so that the power of Christ may reside in me. Therefore I am content with weaknesses, with insults, with troubles, with persecutions and difficulties for the sake of Christ, for whenever I am weak, then I am strong.

Wait, did you catch that? Three key words: perfect, content, and strong. None sounds like a paltry "barely enough." His perfected power, which is a product of His grace plus my weakness, makes me strong. In the story of the rabble-incited quail feed, God demonstrated that He possesses more than enough power to meet the expressed desires of His people. But in the story of the manna as originally intended by God for His people, He demonstrated that His power, coupled with His grace and each individual need, is perfect. That's the point: His sufficient provision is perfect. God's provision is not barely enough; God's provision is *exactly* enough. **God's sufficient provision for us—His Enough for us—is customized to, not limited by, the needs of those He loves.** He loves us so uniquely, so specifically in our weaknesses, that He provides exactly enough of what we need. Our authenticity, including our weaknesses, is an essential part of the equation.

We can be content in our imperfection because perfection is God's half of the equation—not ours.

Not only can we be content in who we are before God—imperfections and all—but we can be content in His perfect provision to cover them. I do not need more than me as I am with my God's sufficient grace to be Enough.

Take a look at Moses. God used Moses' weakness to make Moses strong: because of his lack of confidence in speaking, he would appear "like God" to Pharaoh, complete with his very own prophet named Aaron. God took Moses' greatest insecurity and turned it into the asset he used most influentially for God's purpose in his life. Note: He did not make Moses a great speaker; Moses did not need to be great in his own abilities. He needed to depend on God to provide the Enough he needed in his very moment of greatest weakness. God spoke through Moses and provided Moses with exactly what he needed in each moment to carry out God's purpose.

God didn't want someone else to help deliver His people from Pharaoh; God had created Moses to do it. The circumstances and relationships in Moses' life had prepared him and God promised to tell him exactly what he needed to say in every moment he needed to say something. Moses was not enough. But everything leading up to God's specific purpose in his life had been a gift from God to prepare him for it. And what he did not have, he did not need. Because God provides exactly enough for each of us.

For Such a Time as This

I LOVE HEARING EXAMPLES of regular people living out their life purposes as they present themselves in unique and unexpected ways. Like the story of Moses. It's one of the reasons I also love the story of Esther so much. Her story is one I have frequently considered in my own struggle for contentment and purpose.

For those who are not familiar with it, the story has so very much to offer—too much to do it justice here. Seriously, take the time to read the book of Esther in the Bible. It has more plot twists, intrigue, and suspense than any Hollywood blockbuster. Esther, a Jewish orphan raised by her cousin Mordecai in a foreign land, had been selected and named Queen to King Xerxes. Throughout this whole selection process and afterward, Mordecai sat at the palace gate and directed all of Esther's actions. A bit of a helicopter cousin— you know the type. From the very beginning, he instructed her not to reveal that she was a Jew to anyone. Mordecai proved helpful at the gate, and not just to Queen Esther. At one point, he uncovered a plot to assassinate King Xerxes, which Esther was able to avert. But he was a bit of a troublemaker as well. He refused to bow down to one of the king's top officials, which greatly irritated the official. In response, the crooked official orchestrated the king's unknowing issuance of a decree that all the Jews were to be annihilated on a certain day. It might have been a bit much in response, but the guy was like that. Mordecai protested furiously, as you would expect one about to be annihilated would. He instructed Esther to go before the king and plead on behalf of the Jews. Initially she refused out of fear and self-doubt, reasoning that she would be killed unless the king decided to spare her life, and he had not requested her presence in the last little while. *Please send someone else to do it.* But Mordecai held firm to what he believed she needed to do:

> "Do not think that because you are in the king's house you alone of all the Jews will escape. For if you remain silent at this time, relief and deliverance for the Jews will arise from another place, but you and your father's family will perish. And who knows but that you have come to your royal position for such a time as this?"
>
> Then Esther sent this reply to Mordecai: "Go, gather together all the Jews who are in Susa, and fast for me. Do not eat or drink for three days, night or day. I and my maids will fast as you do. When this is done, I will go to the king, even though it is against the law. And if I perish, I perish."[1]

When I romanticize the story of Esther, I think it would be an honor to be in a "royal" position, with the ability to effect great change. People knew of her; she

---

1 Esther 4:13-16

was important and revered. She had an identity based on her official title as Queen. She didn't have to do laundry and wash dishes. What a cool life purpose that in itself would be.

If I think about the phrases that I would want running through my head as I am charging to seize my larger-than-life destiny someday, Mordecai's final statement is right up there: *for such a time as this!* But man, what a scary position for Esther to be in. She was a scared young woman whose people had recently been targeted by her husband. She had several weaknesses— being young, being secretly Jewish, being a woman in a culture in which they were summoned rather than respected, and being unsure of whether the king's favor remained with her or not. She had reasons to be afraid. She, like another deliverer named Moses, did not feel prepared for the destiny to which she was being called.

How did she prepare for her role as a history-changer? She sought God's enough. She had Mordecai gather her tribe and fast to seek God's will. Esther did not attempt to gather enough by herself, nor did she simply rely on what Mordecai told her to do: night and day, she and her tribe collectively sought Him. Spoiler alert: God showed up. And seriously, God showed off. Within the span of a few days, God orchestrated the public honoring of Mordecai, the humiliation and death of the corrupt official, and the victory of the Jews over their enemies. Esther's not-enoughs plus God's sufficient grace equaled His power perfected. As Mordecai said, God could have done it without her, but He had a history-altering plan for her life and He provided what she needed to accomplish it.

In my struggle to matter and feel like I am doing "enough" with my life, I often look at the romanticized version of Esther's story as an example of what I want. Sometimes I want the validation that I am one of those people who clearly accomplished something big with her life. And by accomplish something big, I mean something more than mundanely working my way through a really big pile of laundry.

But then God reminds me about the essential importance of Mordecai and his behind-the-scenes role in this story. Without the Mordecai Moments in her life, there would be no Queen Esther Destiny. Without Mordecai investing in Esther, imploring Esther to step out in courage, being an example for Esther by stepping out in courage himself, Esther would not have been Esther.

We are all part of the tribe around us, and we build each other up by being who God is calling us to be. He has a specific purpose in each of our callings. For such a time as this, He has called me not to miss the Mordecai Moments of my day: the moments to direct, the moments to encourage, the moments to teach, the moments to protect, and yes, the moments to serve without recognition. For now, my purpose is to sit at the king's gate and be helpful where I can be. Because that's where He has me. **We can find contentment where He calls us to be, and by encouraging and helping others in the purposes for which they are called.**

MY KIND, HUMBLE GREAT-UNCLE SELMER, the twin brother of my Grandpa Helmer, lived his entire life in a home with his sister Hazel (yes, the one who took the bucket loader ride). He spoke with a gravelly voice that became harder to understand following several thyroid surgeries, but the twinkle in his eye spoke the true message in his heart. The minute we, as kids, would walk in the door, he'd invite us on to his lap and bounce us on his knee. The smile our laughter gave him was priceless. He had a great giggle, for an old guy. Selmer lived a simple life. He farmed and loved people.

When he died a few years ago, many of those attending his funeral spoke of his character, his love of Christ, and his kindness toward family and friends. My mom shared a childhood story of Selmer's heart for others. During grade school, at an age when fitting in mattered immensely, my mom needed corrective, orthopedic shoes—the large, thick-soled, clunky, unfashionable shoes worn by "old" people. Selmer had gone along with Mom and her parents to pick up Mom's shoes. Afterward, Mom was too mortified to go out in public with them on her feet, so Selmer stayed in the car with her as her parents ran an errand. As they sat in the car, he noticed a pair of older nuns walking down the street wearing similar shoes, the large heavy shoes visible from under their habits each time they stepped. In a sincere effort to cheer up his grade-school-aged niece, Selmer excitedly, and earnestly, exclaimed, "See dear! Everyone is wearing those kind of shoes!" (I told you comparison with others is not helpful!) The misguided excitement devastated his niece. But his message came from a sweet place in his heart, a place that simply loved his niece and desperately wanted to ease her sadness.

My aunt Grace, Mom's older sister, shared a story

of moving into her first apartment away from home. Uncle Selmer had come along to help with the move. As they got her settled, he couldn't stand the thought of Grace in that apartment all alone at night and worried that she might be lonely. Uncle Selmer didn't have much money, but he went out and bought her a small television so the apartment wouldn't be so quiet during the evening. It wasn't about buying her a television set; Selmer cared about Grace feeling content in her new home.

These are the types of stories people who loved Selmer told of him. They didn't speak to achievements or accolades. He hadn't pursued those things; Selmer simply strived after people. And his people remembered feeling loved. Uncle Selmer epitomized Micah 6:8, "He has showed you, O Man, what is good. And what does the Lord require of you? To act justly and to love mercy and to walk humbly with your God."

God may call some of us to a life in the spotlight, amassing achievements and accolades. And He will call some of us, like my Uncle Selmer, to something seemingly simpler. Uncle Selmer has profoundly influenced my life, in tiny, imperceptible ways, since I was very young. His presence showed me love. His child-like grin showed me joy bubbling within. The stories about him revealed kindness in fleshly form.

I sat in the pew at his small country church during his funeral and listened to the stories other people shared about him. I had heard some of them before, but stories hold more gravity at a funeral, don't they? As I listened to those stories, remembering and reflecting on the man Selmer was, they served as salve that began to restore some of my own contentment that had been salami-sliced away. Moments of seeing God in the everyday can be like that. **Seeing people authentically living out their daily purpose in powerful, and maybe nearly imperceptible ways, not only encourages us to do the same, but shows us that contentment can be found in the broken moments of our never-enough lives.**

When we are who we are, and do what we are called to do, we glorify God. As we journey day by day, depending on Him, we can go about gathering exactly what we need. In whatever He calls us to do, we don't need to have it all together. In fact, it's okay to be a hot mess. He can work with that. We don't need to do or be more. Trust Him. Depend on Him. Be still, and know that He is God. That's Enough.

Epilogue

SOMEONE SUGGESTED THAT I FINISH this book by explaining how I had come to find peace and contentment in my life and for my home. I laughed out loud. It is a natural concluding thought for a book like this, but that is not my story to tell. I struggle with the hypocrisy of putting myself out there as one who has wisdom to offer even as I fail daily to find my contentment—my Enough—in Him. I did not write this book intending to be one whom others should follow. I am not Moses. I want to believe that He called me to speak up and share where I am in hopes that others will be encouraged and drawn to Him.

Truth is, I don't relate well with Moses. I relate better with the Hebrews. I am part of a tribe wandering through the wilderness, wondering what's next. I too easily forget the One who rescued me from slavery and frequently fall into foolish thinking that suggests my old ways may have been better. I compare my circumstances to others' circumstances, not fully knowing either, and allow Satan to salami-slice my contentment as "fairness" eclipses fullness. I forget who the Creator made me uniquely to be. I long for actual nourishment but frequently deplete my energy sources by striving for meat when manna is what I need.

Nevertheless, God continues to redeem me as He did His Hebrews. He did not bring the Hebrews out of slavery and put them immediately into the Promised Land. They journeyed/A long, meandering journey that likely did not feel purposeful at times. God used the journey to accomplish the greater purpose: to teach His people to depend on Him. To remind them that they were His. And when they refused to obey and were pulled back into their old habits and ways of thinking, the manna continued to rain down. He continued to be faithful. He is faithful to me as I journey, too.

The Lord needles me that He has His own purposes with this book, and points out that perhaps I am more like Moses than I thought. Moses didn't want to put himself out there, either. When God gave him a divine calling and purpose, he focused on his shortcomings, as though God could not overcome them. Moses did not feel like enough. But Moses, in all his failings, followed God and led His people out of slavery. After all, Moses was himself a Hebrew, too.

I long for purpose, and strive to matter. God sees that. It's, in part, what He will provide. But my Enough comes not from the worldly importance of anything I might do or accomplish, or even in the accomplishments of my God-given purposes. My Enough comes from the dependence of seeking those

purposes from Him daily, and in the obedience of doing them. I matter because I am a child of the Creator
of the Universe, who knows me and loves me, and He
says I matter. And that's Enough for me.

Words to My Tribe

Geoff, thank you for being Home to me. For a reserved guy of few words, you make an incredible cheerleader. To my kids—thank you for each being uniquely you. I could not love you more. Ben, I'm excited to read your book someday. Jake, you rock the guitar and I love your passion for your favorite things. Drew, you have such a great sense of humor, and when you're around, I know someone has all the details and logistics figured out. And Lily. Daughter, you are fun. You have brought so much more than pink to our family, and your tender-hearted, feisty personality warms my heart daily.

Thank you to our families—we love our family. We love that you have our backs as Geoff and I wander and wonder what we're doing sometimes. What an amazing tribe you all are.

To Mary Ellen, Tracy, Tim, and Cynthia—this book is so much better because of each of you. Thank you for sharing your gifts with me. What a fun little journey you made this.

Bibliography

Benson, Rev. Joseph. *Commentary of the Old and New Testaments*. New York: Carlton & Porter, 1857.

Bostrom, Kathleen Long, and Elena Kucharik. *God Loves You*. Wheaton, IL: Tyndale, 2001.

Driver, S. R. *The Cambridge Bible for Schools and Colleges: Exodus*. Cambridge: Cambridge University Press, 1911.

Henry, Matthew. *Matthew Henry's Concise Commentary*. N.p., 1706.

Lewis, C. S. *The Screwtape Letters*. New York: Harpers Collins, 1942, Copyright restored 1996.

Shirer, Priscilla. *Breathe: Making Room for the Sabbath*. Nashville: Lifeway Press, 2014.

The NIV Study Bible. 10th Anniversary Edition. Grand Rapids: Zondervan Publishing House, 1995.

Townend, Stuart, and Keith Getty. "*In Christ Alone.*" Brentwood: Capitol CMG, 2002.

Warren, Tish Harrison. *Liturgy of the Ordinary*. Downers Grove, IL: InterVarsity Press, 2016.

Wigram, George. *Englishman's Greek Concordance of the New Testament*.